KEYS CUISINE

KEYS CUISINE
Flavors of the Florida Keys

LINDA GASSENHEIMER

With a Foreword by
Jacques Pépin

THE ATLANTIC MONTHLY PRESS
NEW YORK

Published simultaneously in Canada
Printed in the United States of America

Library of Congress Cataloging-in-Publication Data

Gassenheimer, Linda.
Keys cuisine / Linda Gassenheimer; with a foreword by Jacques
Pepin.
Includes index.
1. Cookery—Florida—Florida Keys. I. Title.
TX715.G247 1991   641.59759'41—dc20   90-19749

ISBN 0-87113-540-X (pbk.)

Design by Laura Hammond Hough

Atlantic Monthly Press
841 Broadway
New York, NY 10003

03 04 05 06 07 08 15 14 13 12 11 10 9 8 7

To Harold, James, John, and Charles,
my most faithful supporters,
whose help and ever-present palates guided my efforts.

Contents

Foreword

by Jacques Pépin

When my friend Linda Gassenheimer told me that she was writing a book on the cuisine of the Florida Keys, I thought it particularly fitting for her to do so.

Linda lived in England for several years, where she owned and ran a cooking school, wrote newspaper articles, and published several cookbooks. She settled in Florida upon her return to the States, and immediately fell in love with her surroundings. As a relative newcomer to that part of the country, she brings to this book—along with her thorough knowledge of international as well as national cooking—a fresh outlook that brightens every page.

She gives us a fascinating introduction that includes a short history of the Keys, and discusses generally the food of that region. Her chapter introductions provide further descriptions, as well as comments from the local cooks whose recipes she features.

Linda has combed the Keys accumulating original recipes. After reconstructing these recipes, she has researched them, standardized and simplified them, tested them, and, finally, selected the best examples to show the versatility and depth of Keys cuisine.

There is a unique Cuban influence in the Keys; you can get "bollos," Cuban black-eyed pea fritters, in Key West, but would probably not find them in the Cuban restaurants of Miami. Likewise, the best conch fritters around can be found in the Keys, and Linda gives several recipes for these, along with recipes for conch and black grouper ceviche, mollette, and guacamole made with mamey, a fruit indigenous to the area.

Linda's section on soup covers everything from bisques made with conch to Marker 88's Black Bean Soup, which I enjoyed the last time I was in the Keys.

The chapter on fish and shellfish beautifully extolls the bounty of the Florida seas, which provide some of the best fish and shellfish in the world. There are many recipes for shrimp—Shrimp Boil with Key Lime Mustard Sauce, Spicy Shrimp with Mango, Avocado, and Chardonnay, and Craig's Shrimp Scampi. Also featured are Florida lobster (Manny and Isa's Fried

Lobster), shark (Tugboat's Fried Shark Basket), tuna (Gingered Tuna with Black Bean Relish), wahoo (Grilled Wahoo with Papaya Salsa and Cilantro Butter), frogs' legs (Everglades Frogs' Legs), and even alligator (André's Gator Steak). A few years ago I was in the Keys with my wife for a bonefish tournament. We tasted the very sophisticated cuisine developed there by young Keys chefs at Cheeca Lodge in Islamorada, and witnessed their special way of handling fish native to the area.

The chapter on meat and poultry offers interesting recipes like the Keys Jerk Chicken, Cuban Roast Chicken, Arroz con Pollo, and Edna Howard's Steam.

The desserts are, of course, strong on fruit of the area: Key Lime Pie is featured, naturally, along with an entire repertoire of recipes using this unique citrus fruit. In addition, there are recipes for Duval Café con Leche Cake and Cheeca Lodge Passion Fruit Pie (which my wife and I were privileged to taste when we were there).

Linda demonstrates how different the food in the Upper Keys is from that of the Lower Keys, where the Bahamian and Latin influences are so strong. She introduces us to characters of the area, like Edna Howard, a ninety-one-year-old woman of Bahamian descent who still helps out at church dinners, and a fishing guide named Billy Knowles, a fourth-generation "Conch" whose family had a pineapple plantation on Plantation Key.

Keys Cuisine features some very good simple home cooking and recipes from "hole in the wall" restaurants, as well as from several known restaurants and fine hotels.

This instructive and exciting book is a must for anyone interested in Americana, good cuisine, and that last frontier of cooking, the Florida Keys.

Introduction

The cooking of the Florida Keys has long been due national recognition. For centuries the Keys have been a cross-cultural mecca for pirates, fishermen, artists, writers, and wealthy bons vivants from all over the United States, Cuba, France, England, and the Caribbean. Within this blend of diverse life-styles and backgrounds, a dynamic regional cuisine has been cultivated. The abundant fresh fish and shellfish, tropical fruits, and vegetables of the Keys are the primary ingredients in its cooking. From the hardy down-home recipes of shrimpers and fishing guides to the sophisticated fare of luxury resorts, *Keys Cuisine* documents a remarkable culinary phenomenon.

The history of the Keys, as it was influenced by Europeans, begins in 1513, when Ponce de León first came upon the untamed islands he called Los Mártirs, the martyrs. Soon, they became a landmark for Spanish ships bringing gold and silver from the New World to the Old.

During the Revolutionary War, loyalists who refused to fight against the Crown fled to the Bahamas and then sailed back to Key West, the Keys' southernmost island. Their English style of cooking is still an integral part of Keys cuisine.

During Cuba's War of Rebellion against Spain in 1898, many Cubans crossed the Gulf Stream to Key West. At one time, they made up one-third of Key West's population, and their influence still plays an important role in its cuisine.

Key West, a natural port and refueling station, became the center of the Lower Keys in the nineteenth century. It was at one time the largest city in Florida, and its main industries were maritime-based: fishing, sponging, turtling, and salvaging wrecked ships.

As a seafaring community, Key West cooking took on an international character. Today on Duval Street you can eat an exquisite French Key Lime Tart at a French bistro or a beautiful Conch Salad at a Japanese restaurant. Or you can stop at a stand and snack on bollos and Cuban coffee.

The Upper and Middle Keys developed differently from the Lower Keys. The hard-working Methodist fishermen and farmers who originally settled in this area made their living from the sea and the land. Farmers cleared the land and planted coconuts, pineapples, tomatoes, citrus, and melons. Their harvest was transported by small draft boats to deeper water and loaded onto schooners bound for Key West or the mainland. The sea was the only viable means of transportation until 1912, when Henry Flagler completed the railway that ran from Palm Beach to Key West.

Key West thrived with the introduction of the railroad. Fruits and vegetables shipped in from the Caribbean and South America were loaded onto trains and transported north. The Upper and Middle Keys did not reap such benefits. Farmers could not compete with the cheaper prices of the imported produce, and soon competition and overplanting brought an end to plantation farming in the Keys.

Then on September 2, 1935, a catastrophic hurricane hit Islamorada and Matecumbe Keys: an eighteen-foot tidal wave driven by 250-mile-per-hour winds killed hundreds of people and destroyed the railroad tracks. For three years, until a new road was built along the old track bed, Key West was cut off from the mainland. Even when completed, however, the road was a tenuous link, as ferries were needed where bridges were not yet rebuilt.

Cut off from Key West, the economy of the Upper and Middle Keys was devastated. Commercial and game fishing emerged as the primary sources of employment, and small communities grew up around fishing camps. On these islands there was little to do except fish, drink, and eat. The Green Turtle Inn on Upper Matecumbe had a jukebox. More lively entertainment meant going to Plantation Yacht Harbor or Martin's Halfway House, where there was a piano and, on Saturday nights, a trio from Homestead. There were no drinking-hour restrictions. Jack's Bar was open twenty-four hours a day, seven days a week. During the late fifties and early sixties, no one in the Upper Keys locked their doors. When a restaurateur went out with friends, the restaurant was left open, and whoever came in helped themselves to a drink and left their money on the bar.

The cooking of the Upper and Middle Keys began to take on a character of its own. Over the past twenty years it has been heavily influenced by the chefs of three restaurants: The Conch, Marker 88, and The Green Turtle Inn. Today, classics like Ziggie's Conch Chowder, André Mueller's Snapper Rangoon or Mangoes Morada, and Henry Rosenthal's Turtle Soup can be found on the menus of many restaurants in Key Largo and Islamorada. Manny and Isa have brought the area some of its only Cuban cooking in their small restaurant in Islamorada.

Until recently the Keys were, for the most part, ignored by large developers because of the lack of fresh water. In 1942 the Navy built an eighteen-inch water pipeline that ran 130 miles from Florida City to Key West. The water took a week to travel the route. In 1982 the old pipeline was replaced with a thirty-six-inch line, increasing the volume of water fourfold. Now vacationers from around the world, weekenders from Miami, and settlers looking for a more relaxed life-style have caused a population boom.

In spite of this new influx, there is still a lot of good home cooking going on in the Keys. In the words of an esteemed local chef, "The fish is some of the best you can find in the world, and simple cooking is all it needs."

Keys Cuisine brings you everything from down-home fare to sophisticated culinary gems. Recipes have been gathered from many sources: backcountry fishing guides; commercial fish houses; descendants of the original Keys settlers; guarded secrets, passed along by influential Keys families like the Wolfsons of Key West; and people like Edna Howard, a ninety-one-year-old woman of Bahamian descent and Cuban marriage, who still cooks for church dinners at the Cornish Memorial A.M.E. Zion Church her family helped build. More elaborate recipes are included from many fine Keys resorts and restaurants that use fresh tropical ingredients and multicultural influences to create a sophisticated new type of Keys cuisine.

SNACKS AND DRINKS

My first Keys' sunset was a spectacular event. An unusual cold spell with temperatures in the fifties had descended that Christmas. The sunsets produced by this clear, cool weather were vivid shades of violet, orange, mauve, and pink, framed by swaying palm trees.

There followed the Keys ritual of toasting the sunset accompanied by a few snacks. The most renowned sunset celebration takes place at Mallory Square in Key West. It has become more of a circus than anything else, with flame swallowers, unicyclists, and bands playing. Boaters favor a sunset cruise, where the view of the sun's descent into the sea is uninterrupted. Landlubbers sit on their decks or gather at local restaurants, where music, snacks, and drinks abound.

The Keys snacks featured in this book are fun, delightful recipes that include such local specialties as conch fritters and smoked fish. Several other conch and fish recipes, as well as dishes made with Key West pink shrimp and crab, are included. The three traditional sauces—cocktail, mustard, and tartar sauce—are given in several variations. These sauces can be used interchangeably with many of the recipes throughout the book, according to your preference.

One can't talk about tropical drinks in the area of the Keys without mentioning rum. Sugar cane cultivation and the distillation of "aguardiente" has been part of Caribbean life since the first sugar cane shoots were brought from the Canaries and planted in Cuba. The rough "killer rum" of the sixteenth century became a refined and popular Cuban drink by the mid nineteenth century. During Prohibition, according to *Fortune* magazine, "Havana became the unofficial United States' saloon." Airlines advertised, "Fly to Cuba today and bathe in Bacardi rum." It was only a hop, skip, and jump from Havana to Key West and the rest of the Keys. The wide array of rum-based drinks and the varied uses of rum in Keys cooking reflect the popularity of this ambrosia.

Bring a touch of the tropics into your living room. Enjoy these Keys snacks and drinks and envision the palm trees and sunset for which they were created.

Snacks

Manny and Isa's Conch Fritters with Tomato and Horseradish Cocktail Sauce 7

Monte's Conch Fritters with Mustard Sauce 8

Bollos (using uncooked peas) 9

Bollos (using cooked peas) 10

Conch Ceviche with Sweet-and-Sour Mustard Sauce 11

Black Grouper Ceviche 12

Carriage Trade Garden Key West Shrimp with Tomato and Key Lime Cocktail Sauce 13

Hawk's Cay Shrimp Caribbean 14

Dorothy's Smoked Fish Spread 15

Smoked Marlin Spread 17

Honey and Country Style Grainy Mustard Dip for Smoked Fish 18

Frances Wolfson's Pickled Shrimp 19

Manny and Isa's Conch Fritters with Tomato and Horseradish Cocktail Sauce

Conch fritters are an important part of Keys cooking. These little fried balls of ground conch with vegetables and spices dipped in a cocktail sauce can be found at most bars and restaurants. They're delicious appetizers and can be made ahead, frozen, and warmed when needed. There are those who like light and fluffy conch fritters and those who like firmer ones, filled with lots of conch. Manny and Isa's fritters are famous in the Upper Keys and belong to the firmer variety.

1¼ pounds conch
8 ounces bread crumbs (about 8 slices white bread)
2 eggs
1 medium green pepper, cut into pieces
½ large onion, cut into pieces
2 tablespoons Tabasco sauce

2 tablespoons lime juice
¼ teaspoon salt
¼ teaspoon freshly ground black pepper
¼ teaspoon thyme
1 cup cracker meal
oil for frying

Rinse the conch, cut off the orange fin and the foot, and discard. Cut into pieces and place in the container of a food processor or grinder with the remaining ingredients except the cracker meal and oil. Grind the mixture and remove to a bowl. Wet your hands and roll mixture into 1½- to 2-inch balls. Roll in the cracker meal. Heat oil to 350 degrees and fry fritters a few at a time for about 5 minutes or until golden brown. Drain and serve with cocktail sauce.

Makes around 30 fritters.
10 servings.

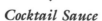

Cocktail Sauce

2 cups catsup   *2 tablespoons horseradish*

Combine the ingredients in a small bowl and taste for seasoning, adding more horseradish if necessary.

Monte's Conch Fritters with Mustard Sauce

At Monte's Seafood in Summerland, conch fritters are cooked to perfection. They are light and fluffy and filled with flavor.

1 pound conch or shrimp
2 red peppers
2 green peppers
2 large onions
1 tablespoon cayenne pepper

2 teaspoons Old Bay Seasoning
1 egg
2½ cups self-rising flour
oil for frying

Rinse the conch and remove and discard the orange fin and the foot. Chop the conch in the container of a food processor. I prefer the vegetables to be coarsely chopped so that there are crunchy pieces in the fritters, so I chop the peppers and onions by hand. Place the chopped conch and vegetables in a bowl, add the seasonings, egg, and mix in the flour. Roll into small balls. Bring the oil to 350 degrees. Add 1 fritter at a time, waiting a few seconds before adding the next. Fry only 5 at a time, removing and adding as they are cooked. (Cooking so few fritters at a time means that the oil is kept at a constant temperature rather than dropping a few degrees each time more food is added. This keeps the fritters crunchy rather than oil-logged.) Fry for 5 minutes or until golden and light. Drain and serve with the mustard sauce.

Makes around 30 fritters.
10 servings.

Mustard Sauce

3 tablespoons mayonnaise
1 tablespoon prepared mustard

1 teaspoon fresh lemon juice
salt and freshly ground black pepper to taste

Mix all of the ingredients together and taste for seasoning. Add salt and pepper to taste.
About ¼ cup sauce.

Bollos (using uncooked peas)

Bollos, also known as *Bollitos de Carita* or *Frituras de Caritas,* are available in Cuban restaurants and small sandwich shops in Key West. These little black-eyed-pea fritters were commonly found in the Chinatown of pre-Castro Havana. Although the recipe is Cuban, it seems to be a specialty of the Latin community in Key West rather than Miami. Bollos can be eaten as a vegetable or for snacks. They're great with beer. Although they are best when just made, they will keep and can be eaten cold or reheated.

The most common form of bollos involves peeling soaked black-eyed peas, then grinding and frying them. Another version involves cooking black-eyed peas until they are soft. This is less time-consuming and produces a flavorful fritter. I have included recipes for each method.

If you're in Key West, stop by 5 Brothers Grocery, a local general store on the corner of Southard and Grinnel. There you can order enough bollos from Herderito Paez for a party, or you can just snack on them right there. Paez, who also sells his mixture frozen, makes fifty pounds of bollos or bollitos a week. He soaks the peas overnight, peels them, grinds them with garlic, salt, and hot pepper sauce, and adds the soaking water until they are fluffy. He cooks them by dropping spoonfuls of the mixture into hot oil.

I confess that I use Herderito's recipe and do not bother to peel the peas. The result, with the use of a food processor to make sure the mixture is smooth, is very good.

2 cups dried black-eyed peas*	½ teaspoon hot pepper sauce
4 cloves garlic, crushed	1 teaspoon salt
2 chili peppers, seeded and finely chopped	oil for frying

Cover the peas with water and soak overnight. Drain, reserving the water. If peeling the peas, rub them in a dish towel to loosen the skins and then place them in a bowl of water. (As mentioned above, this step can be omitted.) Most of the skins will float to the top. Puree the peas in the container of a food processor until as fine as cornmeal (or use a food grinder, which will take several grindings). Add the seasonings and about ½ cup of the soaking water. Beat until the mixture is light, adding additional water if necessary. Heat the oil to 350 degrees and drop in teaspoonfuls (to form 1-inch diameter balls) of the mixture, a few at a time. Deep-fry the bollos for 1 to 2 minutes or until golden brown. Drain on paper towels. You may want to fry one ball first and taste it for seasoning before frying the rest.

Makes about 40 fritters.

*Frozen skinned black-eyed peas can be found in some supermarkets. Use them if you don't have the time to soak the black-eyed peas.

Bollos (using cooked peas)

1½ cups dried black-eyed peas
1 medium onion, sliced
2 cloves garlic, bruised
2 large cloves garlic, crushed

2 chili peppers, seeded and chopped
½ teaspoon salt
½ cup flour
oil for frying

Soak the peas in water to cover overnight. Drain and place in a saucepan with fresh water to cover. Add the sliced onion and bruised garlic. Bring the water to a boil and simmer for about 2 hours or until the peas are soft. Drain well. Puree in a food mill or food processor. Add the crushed garlic, chili peppers, and salt; mix well. Form into 1-inch balls and roll in the flour, shaking off any excess. Heat the oil to 350 degrees and carefully drop the balls in, a few at a time. Fry for about 1 minute or until golden brown. Drain on paper towels and serve.

Makes about 30 fritters.

Conch Ceviche with Sweet-and-Sour Mustard Sauce

André Mueller, Chef de Cuisine at Marker 88, served this appetizer at the Save Our Strength, Taste of the Nation benefit for the hungry. In this case the conch is cut so that it looks something like spaghetti. André says the secret is to keep the onions separate and serve them on top of the ceviche. The sauce can also be served with shrimp or stone crabs.

1½ pounds conch
2 or 3 limes or lemons, juiced

1½ medium red onions, thinly sliced

Trim off all brown or yellow skin from conch. Freeze conch (at least one hour) until slightly stiff to make slicing easier. Slice on a slicing machine, in the food processor, or by hand. Place the sliced conch in a glass bowl and pour the lime juice over it. Refrigerate 4 hours. Taste before serving and add more lime juice if necessary. Serve conch meat topped with sliced onions on a platter with the sweet-and-sour sauce on the side for dipping.

6 servings.

◆

Sweet-and-Sour Mustard Sauce

2½ tablespoons white vinegar
1 tablespoon lemon juice
1 teaspoon dry mustard powder
½ teaspoon Worcestershire sauce

2½ tablespoons water
1¾ cups corn oil
¼ cup honey

Place vinegar, lemon juice, mustard, and Worcestershire sauce in the container of an electric mixer or food processor. Blend well, making sure all lumps are dissolved. Add the water. On medium speed, add the oil, a few drops at a time. The mixture should form a mayonnaise-type sauce. Stir in the honey and mix well. Refrigerate for about 1 hour. Taste and add more lemon juice, if necessary.

6 servings.

Black Grouper Ceviche

There are many varieties of grouper, but they are all white-fleshed. Their skin is tough with a strong flavor so they are usually cooked as fillets rather than whole with the skin. Black Grouper is common in South Florida. It has black skin and snow-white meat. Filleting it is like cutting through butter. Any firm white-fleshed fish can be used for this recipe.

George Trellis, a boner at the Waterfront Market in Key West, used to make this recipe for the market. Although he's no longer there, he carefully taught Charlene Borck, the owner, how to make this popular dish.

2 pounds skinned fillets black grouper	*2 teaspoons oregano*
1 cup lemon juice	*½ teaspoon ground coriander*
⅓ cup lime juice	*¼ cup raw sugar*
2 tablespoons crushed garlic	*¼ cup olive oil*
⅓ large yellow onion, coarsely chopped	*salt and freshly ground black pepper to taste*

Cut the fish into bite-size pieces and marinate in the lemon and lime juice for 1 hour. Add the rest of the ingredients and taste for seasoning, adding more sugar, salt, or pepper as needed. Refrigerate for 24 hours. Serve.

8 servings.

Carriage Trade Garden Key West Shrimp with Tomato and Key Lime Cocktail Sauce

To get to the Carriage Trade Garden, you must first walk through the Carriage Trade Salon, a hairdressing shop. The garden restaurant is only open for lunch. In its center stands a large ficus banyan tree, in which a tree house with charming pink-pelican bannisters is perched. When Bill Gaiser finishes his morning appointments in the hairdressing shop, he rushes to his immaculate kitchen to prepare lunch. Bill opens at night for private parties only. The restaurant is an obvious labor of love for Bill. He works with the very best quality ingredients, serving Key West shrimp when one of the shrimpers calls him to say he has a particularly good catch. His method of cooking the shrimp is also important. The shrimp are always big and juicy when cooked à la Bill.

Key West shrimp, which have pink shells, are large and are very sweet. They retain their pale pink color when cooked. However, any good-quality large shrimp can be served this way.

2 pounds large shrimp　　　　　　　*1 tablespoon Key lime or lemon juice*

Shell the shrimp and devein them by making a slit along the back or outside of the shrimp, lifting out the black vein, and discarding it. Rinse the shrimp and place them in a pot of water, along with the Key lime juice, making sure the water covers the shrimp. Bring to a simmer with the bubbles just starting around the edge of the pot; the water will start to turn white. Take off the heat and let sit 1 minute. Then drain the shrimp and plunge them into a bowl of ice water. Drain again and serve with the cocktail sauce.

6 servings.

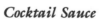

Cocktail Sauce

½ cup catsup　　　　　　　　　*1 teaspoon chili sauce*
1 tablespoon Key lime or lemon juice　　*1 teaspoon Worcestershire sauce*

Combine the ingredients in a small bowl and taste for seasoning, adding more Worcestershire or chili sauce as necessary. Spoon into a serving bowl and serve with the shrimp.

Makes about ½ cup sauce.

Hawk's Cay Shrimp Caribbean

Hawk's Cay Resort and Marina is beautifully situated on the five islands of Duck Key at mile marker 61. These coconut-covered shrimp are served as appetizers or a main course in their Caribbean Room. The Horseradish Marmalade Sauce is easy to make and can be used as a dip for chicken, pork, or beef.

*1½ cups flour
1 teaspoon salt
¼ teaspoon white pepper
2 egg yolks, beaten
¾ cup flat beer*

*1 tablespoon dark rum
24 large shrimp*
1 cup sweetened coconut flakes
oil for frying*

Mix the flour, salt, pepper, and egg yolks in a bowl. Gradually add the beer and rum, stirring to thoroughly blend the ingredients. Cover and allow the batter to rest in the refrigerator for 1 to 2 hours. Shell the shrimp and devein them by making a slit along the back or outside of the shrimp, lifting out the black vein, and discarding it. Rinse, pat dry, and dip the shrimp in batter. Roll the shrimp in coconut flakes. Heat oil in pan for deep frying to 350 degrees. Slip one shrimp at a time into the oil, cooking only about 3 or 4 shrimp at a time. Fry 1 to 2 minutes or until golden brown. Drain on paper towels. Serve on toothpicks with dipping sauce.

6 servings.

◆

Horseradish Marmalade Sauce

1 cup orange marmalade

¼ cup prepared horseradish

Mix the marmalade and horseradish together and place in a serving or dipping bowl.
Makes about 1¼ cups sauce.

*You can substitute chicken strips cut to about the same size as shrimp.

Dorothy's Smoked Fish Spread

When Dorothy Hertel started the Islamorada Fish Company, the company smoked its own fish. Now it is too busy for this delicate and time-consuming process. Claudette Becker, a local woman whose husband fishes for Dorothy, smokes the fish now. It's an expensive process, especially since a fish shrinks by one-third of its original size when smoked. Claudette guards her smoking secrets. The fish is soaked overnight in a brine solution made up of salt, spices, and brown sugar. Her husband, Warren, developed the brine recipe and built their two smoke houses, which are eight feet tall and look like large dressers. Each has seven drawers with racks that hold the fish. Claudette smokes amberjack that her husband catches throughout the winter. At other times she smokes kingfish, dolphin, and marlin. The heat comes from the bottom, and the drawers are rotated during the 8- to 10-hour smoking processes. She uses buttonwood and pine for the fire. Since it is illegal in the Keys to cut buttonwood trees down, Claudette trades Warren's catch of lobster and stone crabs for the county's buttonwood that is gathered when the trees are pruned.

Dorothy lives in an old Conch house right next to the Fish Company. It's made of old Dade county pine that is so hard it won't take nails, and is impervious to termites. Dorothy says they

have to use a drill and screws when they do any renovations. They can sit on their deck and watch the perfect Keys sunsets and munch on some of her smoked fish appetizers. While I was there, the sponge men in their little skiffs and flat-bottomed boats were just coming in, their boats loaded with sponges.

2 pounds smoked fish (any type will do)
6 ounces cream cheese
1 tablespoon mayonnaise
1 tablespoon chopped onion

1 dash Tabasco sauce
1 teaspoon Worcestershire sauce
1 teaspoon lemon juice

Place the fish, cream cheese, mayonnaise, and onion in the bowl of a food processor and process well. (If not using a food processor, flake the fish with a fork and mix in the cream cheese, mayonnaise, and onion.) Add the Tabasco, Worcestershire, and lemon juice. Taste and add more seasoning as necessary. Use as an appetizer, dip, or spread.

8 servings as an appetizer; 16 as a dip or spread.

♦

Smoked Fish Ideas

Slice smoked fish into bite-sized pieces and dip into Mustard Sauce used for Ziggie's Stone Crabs (page 89). Smoked Conch is hard to find, but delicious. If you do come across some, shave it into very thin pieces and eat as is. It's great served with drinks and doesn't need a dip.

Smoked Marlin Spread

The Waterfront Market on Williams Street has a beautiful display of fresh fish and prepared fish dishes. Charlene Borck smokes her fresh marlin over hickory wood. The secret of her Smoked Marlin Spread is that it is packed with the hickory-smoked fish.

Use this spread as a dip with crackers or vegetables, or on toast; or fill small pastry shells for more formal hors d'oeuvres.

*1 pound smoked marlin (other smoked fish
  may be used)*
½ cup sweet pickle relish
¼ cup prepared horseradish
¼ cup chopped onion

½ teaspoon lime juice
1 teaspoon hot pepper sauce
⅔ cup mayonnaise
salt and freshly ground black pepper to taste

Coarsely chop the fish and place in a mixing bowl. Add the relish, horseradish, onion, and lime juice; mix well. Add half the hot pepper sauce and half the mayonnaise. Blend together and taste. Add more hot sauce according to your taste. Add salt and pepper to taste. The mayonnaise should just barely hold the mixture together. Add more as needed.

6 to 8 servings.

Honey and Country Style Grainy Mustard Dip for Smoked Fish

Karole Rispoli makes this dip for her husband's Raw Bar at the Ocean Key House in Key West. The sweet and hot sauce is perfect with smoked fish. They use smoked amberjack at the Bar, but any smoked fish cut into chunks is fine. The sauce is great with conch fritters, stone crab claws, steamed crabs, or cooked shrimp.

1 cup mayonnaise
½ cup country-style grainy mustard

⅓ cup honey
2 teaspoons Key lime juice

Combine the ingredients in a small bowl and taste for seasoning, adding more mustard or honey if necessary.

6 to 8 servings
Makes about 2 cups sauce.

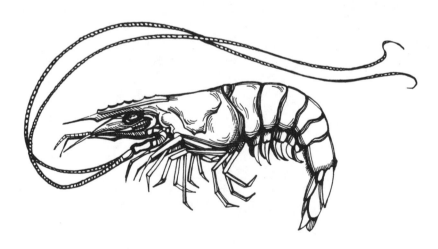

Frances Wolfson's Pickled Shrimp

Frances Louise Cohen of Pensacola, a fourth-generation Floridian whose great-grandfather fought for the Confederacy, married Colonel Mitchell Wolfson, Sr., in 1926. By 1900 the Wolfson family operated the Store of Fashion at 716 Duval Street, having come to Key West in 1887. Although the family moved to Miami in 1915, they kept their ties with Key West and spent much of their vacation time there.

Frances's son Mitchell Wolfson, Jr., invited me to explore his mother's recipe box. Pickled Shrimp is a recipe from her collection. It can be made two days ahead and makes a delicious Keys hors d'oeuvre.

⅔ cup corn or safflower oil	*1 teaspoon dry mustard*
⅔ cup white vinegar	*3 bay leaves*
2 limes, juiced	*½ teaspoon cayenne pepper*
1½ tablespoons sugar	*2 pounds shrimp*
1 teaspoon dill seeds	*½ large onion, sliced*
1 teaspoon cracked black peppercorns	*½ cup chopped fresh cilantro*

Combine the ingredients, except the shrimp, cilantro, and onion, in a saucepan and bring to a boil; simmer for 10 minutes. While the sauce is simmering, peel the shrimp and devein them by making a slit along the back or outside of the shrimp, lifting out the black vein, and discarding it. Rinse the shrimp and add them to the saucepan. Simmer very gently for 3 minutes (the shrimp will become rubbery if they are brought to a hard boil). Drain the shrimp, reserving the cooking marinade. In a large bowl, layer the onion slices and the shrimp, alternating until both are used up. Sprinkle the cilantro into the reserved hot marinade and pour over the mixture. Cover tightly with plastic wrap. Chill for about 48 hours.

Remove the shrimp from the marinade and serve on wooden picks, or slice and place on pumpernickel rounds decorated with fresh cilantro leaves.

6 hors d'oeuvre servings.

Shrimp Mousse

This recipe was inspired by Margaret Dicker's prize-winning shrimp dish at the Key Largo Island Jubilee Cook-Off. Her unusual method of cooking the shrimp ensures that they are juicy and not overcooked. The fresh taste of the shrimp combined with fresh herbs and vegetables makes this a tempting dish to have with drinks while watching the sun set. It will keep 2 days in the refrigerator and can be served as a luncheon or buffet dish.

½ pound fresh shrimp
2 cups water
1 envelope unflavored gelatin
1¼ cups tomato juice
6 ounces cream cheese
½ cup finely chopped green pepper
1 stick celery, finely diced

2 tablespoons finely chopped onion
¼ cup finely chopped fresh cilantro or parsley
1 cup mayonnaise
salt and freshly ground black pepper to taste
fresh cilantro or parsley
1 quart mold, lightly oiled

Shell the shrimp and devein them by making a slit along the back or outside of the shrimp, lifting out the black vein, and discarding it. Bring the 2 cups water to a rolling boil. Remove from the heat and add the shrimp. Leave the shrimp in the water until the water cools, allowing them to cook gently. Drain the shrimp, reserving ¼ cup of the water, and cut them into ½-inch pieces. Add the gelatin to the ¼ cup water and let soften. Pour the tomato juice into another saucepan and heat gently. Melt the cream cheese in the juice and add the softened gelatin. Strain and set aside to cool. Mix the shrimp with the tomato juice, green pepper, cilantro, celery, and onion. Add salt and pepper to taste. Stir the mayonnaise into the cooled tomato juice mixture. Taste for seasoning once more. Pour into mold and refrigerate until set.

To serve, unmold and decorate with fresh cilantro or parsley.

8 to 10 servings.

Crabby Cheese Dip

Margaret Dicker made this delicious dip for the Island Jubilee Cook-Off in Key Largo. Restaurateurs and locals both come to the cook-off once a year to display their best dishes. It has become a big event in the Upper Keys and everyone eagerly looks forward to tasting the entries.

This is a great way to use leftover crabmeat. It's simple to make and very good. You can use canned crab, but use the best quality you can find. This has more the texture of a quiche than of a dip or spread. Make it to go with drinks, for a lunch entrée, or as a first course.

¾ pound cooked fresh crabmeat or 2 cans crabmeat (6 ounces each)
1 cup grated Swiss cheese
1 cup finely chopped onion
1 cup mayonnaise

1 teaspoon nutmeg
salt and freshly ground black pepper to taste
6 cup soufflé dish or equivalent size oven-proof dish

Preheat oven to 350 degrees. Drain the crabmeat and combine with the remaining ingredients in a large bowl. Taste for seasoning, adding more nutmeg, salt, or pepper as needed. Spoon into the soufflé dish and bake for 30 minutes. Serve hot in same dish, with crackers or crusty bread.

8 servings.

Fried Crab Fingers

Blue crabs are plentiful throughout the Keys. The white lump meat from the body is used in many recipes and the claws are a delicacy whether steamed or fried. To get the meat from the claws, steam the crabs (see Steamed Blue Crabs, page 87) and twist off the claws. You want to remove the shell leaving the pincers on and the meat intact. Place the point of a strong sharp knife on the shell and gently tap with a hammer. The shell will crack and you can remove the meat. The pincer remains to act as a handle.

2 pounds cooked blue crab claws
2 eggs
1 cup cornmeal
1 cup flour

½ teaspoon salt
¼ teaspoon freshly ground black pepper
oil for frying

Shell the crab claws. In a small bowl lightly beat the eggs with a few drops of water to form an egg wash. Combine the cornmeal, flour, salt, and pepper in a second bowl. Dip the crab claws in the egg wash and then roll in the flour mixture. Heat the oil in a large pan or deep-fryer to 350 degrees. Drop 3 or 4 claws into the oil and fry for about 3 minutes or until golden. Remove and drain on paper towels. Continue cooking in this manner until all of the claws are cooked. Serve with cocktail sauce (page 7, 13, or 29).

6 servings.

The Pier House Conch Egg Rolls

Michael Kulow, executive chef, has taken an oriental dish and given it a Keys touch, using conch, cilantro, and hot peppers. Egg roll skins can be found in two different sizes in the frozen section of supermarkets. Use the large ones as a first course or luncheon dish and the small size for hors d'oeuvres or snacks. Egg rolls taste best when freshly made, but they will reheat in the oven the next day. Be sure to leave space around each one and turn them once during the warming to make sure the skin stays crisp. Shrimp may be substituted for conch.

⅓ cup sesame oil
2 Jalapeño peppers, seeded and chopped
2 tablespoons chopped fresh ginger
2 scallions, chopped
1 tablespoon crushed garlic
½ cup dry sherry
1 pound conch, finely chopped
½ cup chopped mushrooms (about 2 ounces)
½ bunch fresh cilantro, chopped
2 tablespoons rice vinegar
2 tablespoons oyster sauce

1 tablespoon Tamari soy sauce
salt and freshly ground black pepper to taste
1½ cups shredded green cabbage
1½ cups shredded purple cabbage
2 tablespoons rice vinegar
2 tablespoons Tamari soy sauce
¾ cup bean sprouts, chopped
¾ cup sliced snow peas
15 egg roll skins
peanut oil for frying

Pour half the sesame oil into a skillet and sauté the peppers, ginger, scallions, and garlic until soft. Deglaze the pan with sherry, scraping up any brown bits. Add conch and mushrooms to the sherry and cook until the liquid is absorbed. Remove from heat and add cilantro, 2 tablespoons rice vinegar, oyster sauce, and 1 tablespoon Tamari, and season with salt and pepper to taste. Toss the two cabbages together with the remaining sesame oil and 2 tablespoons each of rice vinegar and Tamari. Add the bean sprouts and snow peas. Add the conch mixture to the vegetables and mix well. Line up the egg roll wrappers on a countertop and place a spoonful of the mixture on a corner of each one. Roll up, tucking in the corners as you go, to form a 6-inch by 1-inch roll.

To fry, heat the oil to 350 degrees and add the rolls one at a time, turning them as they cook. Fry about 3 rolls at a time to ensure that the oil stays at a frying temperature. Cook until golden brown, about 1½ minutes. Drain on paper towels and serve.

Makes 15 large rolls.

Mollette

When Bobbie Sawyer was a child she used to go with her grandparents on Sundays to help sell snacks at the cock fights. She remembers these mollettes being very popular. Cuban bread is filled with picadillo, sealed in egg wash, rolled in cracker meal, and deep fried. Many people in Key West spell this *moyette,* but Bobbie's family spells it the Spanish way. In either case, it is a good snack, especially if you have some leftover picadillo. Any type or size of oblong bread or roll can be used for this recipe. Simply adjust the amount of picadillo needed.

1 loaf Cuban bread	*2 tablespoons water*
4 cups picadillo (page 145)	*1 cup cracker meal*
1 egg	*oil for frying*

Cut off one end of the bread and set aside. Pull out the center, leaving a border of about 1 inch. Fill the inside with picadillo and replace the cut off end of the bread to seal in the filling; hold together with wooden toothpicks. Mix the egg and water and dip the bread in the wash. Roll in cracker meal. Heat the oil to 350 degrees and fry the bread until golden brown. Slice in 2-inch pieces and serve for snacks.

Makes about 15 pieces.

Plantain Chips, or Marquitas

When you enter a Cuban or Latin restaurant, order some marquitas, or plantain chips, to munch on as you look over the menu. They're great with beer or sangria.

Plantains are larger and greener than bananas. When green, the plantain is starchy with very little flavor. They fry beautifully at this stage. As the plantain turns yellow and ripens, it takes on more of the flavor of a sweet banana, but it holds its shape better than a banana when cooked. To peel a plantain, take a knife and slit the skin along the plantain's natural ridges. Then peel the strips away. For the best results, cut your plantains paper thin and fry the slices for only a minute.

4 green plantains	*salt to taste*
oil for frying	

Peel and thinly slice the plantains. Pour the oil in a pan for deep frying and heat to about 350 degrees. Fry several slices at a time for about 1 minute or until they are golden. Do not let them brown. Add more slices as the first ones get done. Drain on paper towels, sprinkle with salt, and serve.

6 servings.

Sweet Mango Chutney Roulade

"Don't leave out Susan and Laurie's famous chutney roulade," was a request from my friend Kitty Clements. Susan Craig and Laurie Richards have a very popular catering company in Key West, and one of their most successful recipes is this chutney roulade. They make their chutney with ripe mangoes, which they puree and make into a thick paste for spreading.

1 ripe mango, peeled and pitted (see Glossary)
¼ cup raisins
1 tablespoon sweetened flaked coconut
2 teaspoons Chinese hot oil (also known as red
oil, chili oil, and hot pepper oil)
¼ pound roast Cuban pork,* thinly sliced
3 ounces cream cheese

Chop mango and place in a sieve to drain. Add the raisins, coconut, and oil to the mango and puree in the container of a food processor, or chop to a paste by hand. Lay the slices of pork on a countertop and spread with a thin layer of cream cheese. Spread the chutney on top and roll up the slices. Wrap each slice in plastic wrap and refrigerate for 1 hour. Remove the wrap and slice on the diagonal; serve with French bread croutons. The roulades will keep in their wrap in the refrigerator for a day.

Makes approximately 20 roulades.

French Bread Croutons

1 loaf French bread, diagonally sliced
4 tablespoons butter (½ stick)

Heat the butter in a skillet and sauté the croutons on both sides until they just begin to turn golden, adding more butter if needed. Drain and serve with the roulades.

*See Manny and Isa's Cuban Pork Roast (page 147) or use roast pork shoulder.

Guava Shells and Cream Cheese

Fresh guavas are grown in small quantities in Florida but are difficult to find in other parts of the United States. They are usually sold in cans as guava shells or as a paste. According to Elizabeth Schneider in *Uncommon Fruits and Vegetables,* they have an "intense aroma which may, depending on the fruit's ripeness, seem to emanate from either a locker room or the garden of Eden." Their strong flavor and bright orange-red color makes them a perfect addition to desserts, soups, stews, or sauces.

Mary Spottswood in Key West uses guava shells and cream cheese as an hors d'oeuvre with drinks or as a dessert. This makes a pretty platter for a cocktail party.

8 ounces cream cheese   *Cuban crackers (or any nonsalty cracker)*
2 16-ounce cans guava shells

Soften the cream cheese and place in the center of a serving platter. Drain the guava shells and cut into 1- to 2-inch pieces. Arrange around the cheese. Arrange the crackers around the guava and serve. Guests will spread a cracker with some cheese and top it with a piece of guava.
10 servings for drinks.

Alternative suggestion: spread crackers with cream cheese and top with a square of guava paste (see Glossary).

Mamey Guacamole

Tropical fruits rarely heard of outside the Caribbean area are beginning to make their way to wider markets. Until recently, mamey milk shakes served in Cuban restaurants in Key West had been the only popular use for the fruit. The growing interest in tropical fruits, however, has been accompanied by a spate of tempting new recipes. Native to South America, this unusual fruit has a soft, salmon-pink flesh and a rough, russet-brown skin. Some say it tastes like sweet pumpkin, while true devotees say no other fruit can compare with it. Mamey has a texture similar to an avocado, but a flesh that does not oxidize. It therefore makes a delicious guacamole that will not turn dark.

1 medium-sized ripe mamey	*2 tablespoons red wine vinegar*
1 large tomato	*1 tablespoon Worcestershire sauce*
½ medium onion	*salt and freshly ground black pepper to taste*
½ jalapeño pepper	

Cut the mamey in half and scoop out the pulp. Remove the stem and quarter the tomato. Chop the onion in the bowl of a food processor or by hand. Add the mamey and tomato to the onion and chop in the food processor or by hand. Add the remaining ingredients. Taste for seasoning, adding more vinegar or Worcestershire as necessary. Serve as a dip with tortilla chips.

6 appetizer servings.

Marc Green's Tartar Sauce

Marc Green uses this tartar sauce for his fish sandwiches at the Holiday Isle Restaurant.

2 cups mayonnaise
⅓ cup relish
2 tablespoons capers, finely chopped
2 tablespoons finely chopped onion

2 teaspoons Worcestershire sauce
1 teaspoon Tabasco sauce
2 teaspoons lemon juice
salt and freshly ground black pepper to taste

Combine the ingredients in a small bowl and taste for seasoning, adding more as necessary.
6 to 8 servings.
Makes about 2½ cups sauce.

Marker 88 Cocktail Sauce

Marker 88 serves this very simple sauce with its shrimp. It is the sauce André Mueller served with Key West Pink Shrimp when President Bush was fishing in the Keys.

1 cup chili sauce

2 tablespoons prepared horseradish*

Combine the two ingredients in a small bowl, adding more horseradish if you like a hot sauce.
6 servings.
Makes about 1 cup sauce.

*Alter the amount of horseradish used by the heat of the chili sauce chosen.

Drinks

Tiki John's Rum Runner

The smell of the salt air, the uninterrupted ocean view, and the gentle tropical breeze made the perfect setting for John and Lois Ebert's Tiki Bar. They came to the Keys in 1971 and started managing the Tiki Bar at the Holiday Isle Hotel in 1972. Tiki John became one of the favorite bartenders of the Middle Keys and the Tiki Bar, with its old thatched roof and driftwood furniture, became famous. The Chicago *Daily News* listed it as one of the top ten bars in the world.

John and Lois started out by running a do-it-yourself bar. John would set out miniature bottles of liquor on the bar with many kinds of condiments and mixes. You bought a cup and some ice and then went and made your own drink. People started flooding the bar. It was hard to find a place to dock your boat on a nice weekend, and if you were the first one in, you couldn't get out. Soon the Eberts were so busy that they couldn't wait for the customers to make their own drinks, and they started bartending.

At that point John realized that he had inherited too much inventory from the previous manager—his storeroom had too much banana liqueur and blackberry brandy. He mixed these together with some rum and Key limes and invented the famous Rum Runner. Tiki John's Rum Runner is a happy drink that is served all over the Keys. Here is John's original recipe.

⅞ ounce blackberry brandy
⅞ ounce banana liqueur
¾ ounce 151 Rum

⅝ ounce grenadine
1½ ounces lime juice (Key lime if possible)

Fill a blender container three-quarters full with cracked ice or small ice cubes. Add the ingredients and blend until smooth. Serve in a 12-ounce Collins glass.

1 serving.

The Ocean Reef Club's Planter's Punch

The Ocean Reef Club sits at the northern point of Key Largo. Its three golf courses, tennis courts, and marina, and its accessibility to snorkeling and fishing in the Upper Keys have made it a favorite spot for vacationers around the world. It was originally founded in 1945 as a private fishing club. Soon after, a small hotel was built there, and then a few small villas. The number of homes grew into what is now a large fishing and boating community.

Sitting at the Buccaneer Island pool looking out over the bay with the luxury yachts passing by, you will be served this delicious planter's punch by waitresses on roller skates.

1 ounce white rum	*grenadine for color*
3 ounces unsweetened pineapple juice	*Myers's dark rum*
3 ounces orange juice	*1 maraschino cherry*

Fill a 12-ounce glass with ice. Add the white rum, then the pineapple, orange, and grenadine juices. Stir well. Float Myers's rum on top, garnish with maraschino cherry, and serve.

1 serving.

The Quay's Piña Colada

Rum, pineapple, and coconut are three tropical ingredients that were made for each other. Put them together, serve slightly frozen, and you have one of the Keys most famous drinks, the Piña Colada. The Quay restaurant in Key Largo serves their Piña Colada at their outdoor bar looking out over the Gulf of Mexico.

¼ cup unsweetened pineapple chunks *2 shots* unsweetened pineapple juice*
¼ cup Coco Lopez cream of coconut *½ shot* dark rum*
1 cup cracked ice cubes *1 slice fresh pineapple*
2 shots* light rum *2 maraschino cherries*

Mix the pineapple chunks and coconut cream together in the container of a blender. To the pineapple mix, add the ice cubes, light rum, and pineapple juice. Blend until smooth. Pour into two 12-ounce glasses. Float the dark rum on top of each glass. Cut the pineapple slice in half and place each half on a pick along with a cherry. Make a slit in each pineapple slice and balance on the edge of each glass.

2 servings.

*One shot equals 1¼ ounces.

The Pier House Piña Colada Base

The Beach Club Bar at The Pier House in Key West serves an entire assortment of colorful frozen drinks. Overlooking the ocean, it has a perfect setting for a tropical bar. What makes the club's drinks special is they all use a piña colada base that can be easily prepared at home. Make a batch of the base and have a Tropical Piña Colada Party; let your guests select whatever flavor piña colada strikes their fancy.

2 15-ounce cans Coco Lopez cream of coconut   *60 ounces unsweetened pineapple juice*

Combine the ingredients in a gallon jug. The base keeps refrigerated for about 1 week.
Makes 45 drinks.

The Pier House Berry Peachy

This is a raspberry-peach-flavored piña colada.

½ canned peach	*1 slice peach*
½ ounce Chambord raspberry liqueur	*1 slice pineapple*
1 ounce light rum	
2 ounces The Pier House Piña Colada Base	
(page 36)	

Half fill a blender container with ice. Add the ½ peach, liquors, and base and blend. (Running the blender with the ice and ingredients will produce a frozen drink. There should be no ice cubes remaining and the mixture should be thick and smooth.) Serve in a 12-ounce glass. Garnish with peach and pineapple slices.

1 serving.

The Pier House Blue Heron

This is an orange-flavored Piña Colada that is blue.

2 ounces blue curaçao	*2 ounces The Pier House Piña Colada Base*
1 ounce light rum	*(see page 36)*
	1 slice orange

Half fill a blender container with ice. Add liquors and base and blend. (Running the blender with the ice and ingredients will produce a frozen drink. There should be no ice cubes remaining and the mixture should be thick and smooth.) Serve in a 12-ounce glass. Garnish with a slice of orange.

1 serving.

The Pier House Guava Grande

This is a guava-flavored Piña Colada.

½ inch guava paste (comes in a box 2½ inches
wide × ¾ inches high)
1 ounce light rum

2 ounces The Pier House Piña Colada Base
(see page 36)
1 small red hibiscus flower

Half fill a blender container with ice. Add the guava paste, rum, and base and blend. (Running the blender with the ice and ingredients will produce a frozen drink. There should be no ice cubes remaining and the mixture should be thick and smooth.) Serve in a 12-ounce glass. Garnish with hibiscus flower.

1 serving.

The Pier House Peachy Parrot

½ canned peach*
1 ounce rum

2 ounces The Pier House Piña Colada Base
(see page 36)
1 slice peach

Half fill a blender container with ice. Add the ½ peach, rum, and base and blend. (Running the blender with the ice and ingredients will produce a frozen drink. There should be no ice cubes remaining and the mixture should be thick and smooth.) Serve in a 12-ounce glass. Garnish with a peach slice.

1 serving.

*For a stronger peach flavor, add 2 more peach halves.

The Pier House Raspberry Rendezvous

This is a raspberry-flavored Piña Colada.

1 ounce Chambord raspberry liqueur
1 ounce light rum

2 ounces The Pier House Piña Colada Base
  (see page 36)
1 slice pineapple

Half fill a blender container with ice. Add Chambord, rum, and base and blend. (Running the blender with the ice and ingredients will produce a frozen drink. There should be no ice cubes remaining and the mixture should be thick and smooth.) Serve in a 12-ounce glass. Garnish with a slice of pineapple.

1 serving.

The Pier House Orange Gable

This is an almond-flavored piña colada.

1½ ounces amaretto liqueur
2 ounces The Pier House Piña Colada Base
  (see page 36)

splash of orange juice
1 slice orange

Half fill a blender container with ice. Add the amaretto and base and blend. (Running the blender with the ice and ingredients will produce a frozen drink. There should be no ice cubes remaining and the mixture should be thick and smooth.) Serve in a 12-ounce glass. Garnish with a slice of orange.

1 serving.

Hog's Breath Mango Mama

The fleshy orange pulp and fragrant aroma of mangoes make them a perfect flavoring agent for a liqueur. The Hog's Breath Saloon uses Suntory Mohala mango liqueur for this shooter-size refreshing drink with a flowery, fragrant aftertaste.

½ ounce vodka
½ ounce mango liqueur

⅓ cup orange juice

Fill a 12-ounce shaker glass with ice. Add the vodka, mango liqueur, and orange juice and shake well. Strain immediately into a 3½-ounce glass; do not let the drink sit on the ice.

1 serving.

Hog's Breath Shooter Orange Crush

The Hog's Breath shooter drinks are different from most of the drinks in Key West. They are shaken rather than blended and are very refreshing.

½ ounce vodka
½ ounce Triple Sec (orange liqueur)

⅓ cup orange juice

Fill a shaker glass with ice and pour in all of the ingredients. Shake until frothy and strain immediately into a 3½-ounce shooter cup.

1 serving.

Hog's Breath Key Lime Shooter

The Hog's Breath Saloon on Front Street in Key West is a packed saloon. Paige, the bartender, served us one of the most refreshing drinks I've had, explained how it was made, and served everyone else around us without missing a beat. A shooter is a 3½-ounce drink served in a small shooter cup. The drink should be served immediately; do not let it sit on the ice.

This tastes like a Key Lime Pie in a shooter glass. The Spanish liqueur used in the drink is a pleasant mixture of light orange and vanilla flavors. Substitute Cointreau, Grand Marnier, or Triple Sec if you can't find Licor 43.

½ ounce light rum
½ ounce Licor 43 (Spanish orange liqueur, Guarentez Tres)
2 teaspoons Rose's Lime Juice

¼ cup sour mix (Mr. and Mrs. T's)
2 teaspoons orange juice
1 ounce half-and-half

Fill a 16-ounce shaker glass with ice and pour in all of the ingredients. Shake well, place strainer over shaker, and immediately pour into a shooter cup.

1 serving.

Hawk's Cay Bushwacker

President Bush's visit to the Florida Keys just before his inauguration in January 1989 inspired Hawk's Cay Resort and Marina to develop their own Hawk's Cay Bushwacker drink. The resort has a presidential history. Presidents Harry S. Truman, Dwight D. Eisenhower, and Lyndon B. Johnson have stayed at this beautiful spot on Duck Key at mile marker 61. Melon liqueur gives this drink its very special flavor.

If you prefer frozen drinks, combine the ingredients in a blender container half filled with ice. Blend until thick and serve.

¼ shot* light rum
¾ shot* Midori (melon liqueur)
splash of banana liqueur

splash of blue curaçao
unsweetened pineapple juice

Fill a 12-ounce glass with ice cubes and add the rum, Midori, banana liqueur, and blue curaçao. Add enough pineapple juice to fill the glass. Stir and serve.

1 serving.

Poinciana

This pretty thirst-quenching drink is served at La Te Da in Key West.

½ cup champagne
¼ cup Chambord raspberry liqueur
¼ cup cranberry juice

¼ slice pineapple
1 strawberry

Fill a large wine glass with ice and add the champagne, Chambord, and cranberry juice. To garnish, make a slit in the pineapple slice and stick it on the rim of the glass. Place the strawberry on a pick and float it in the drink.

1 serving.

*One shot equals 1¼ ounces.

"Safe" Sex in the Afternoon

Sex in the Afternoon was a selection on the drink menu at La Te Da, La Terraza de Marti, restaurant in Key West. Sitting around the pool, which is in the center of the restaurant, on a bright sunny afternoon I thought, "How can I pass up a drink like that?" When it came to the table it was garnished with a half slice of orange, a strawberry on a toothpick, and a small package at the top of the toothpick. "It's a condom," shouted my luncheon partner. No one in the restaurant even turned around. The manager came over to explain that they had changed the name of the drink to "Safe" Sex in the Afternoon. Hence, the extra garnish. Of course, passion fruit is the main ingredient.

½ cup white rum
¼ cup unsweetened pineapple juice
¼ cup Alize passion fruit liqueur
¼ cup passion fruit juice

½ slice of orange
1 strawberry
1 condom (optional)

Fill a 16-ounce glass with ice. Pour the liquid ingredients over the ice. Make a slit in the orange slice and stick it on the rim of the glass. Place the strawberry on a pick and float it in the drink.

1 serving.

Louie's Passion

I have extolled the virtues of the chef at Louie's Backyard, but Justin, the bartender, makes you feel equally welcome with this special drink. I enjoyed it while sitting in Louie's Backyard watching the sun go down.

1¼ ounces light rum
1½ ounces unsweetened pineapple juice
1½ ounces orange juice
1½ ounces cranberry juice

⅛ inch champagne
½ slice orange
1 maraschino cherry

Fill an 8-ounce wine glass three-quarters full with ice. Add the rum, pineapple juice, orange juice, and cranberry juice. Float ⅛ inch of champagne on top. Do not stir. To garnish, make a slit in the orange and stick on the rim of the glass. Float the cherry in the drink.

1 serving.

Louie's Backyard Banini Aruba

The pale colors of this drink belie its potent contents. With the gentle breezes blowing and the beautiful ocean in front of us on the three-tiered deck at Louie's Backyard in Key West, it was easy to enjoy this delicious drink.

1½ ounces vodka
1½ ounces whiskey
1½ ounces orange juice
1½ ounces unsweetened pineapple juice

splash of freshly squeezed lime juice
splash of grenadine
½ slice orange
1 maraschino cherry

Pour the liquid ingredients into a shaker glass and shake well. Fill a collins glass with ice and pour in the drink. To garnish, make a slit in the orange slice and stick on the rim of the glass. Float the cherry in the drink.

1 serving.

Peppermint Soda

"At the foot of the sun, In the heart of the fun" heads the drinks menu at the Dockside Bar at the Ocean Key House in Key West. The bar deck backs onto Mallory Square so you can stand at the wall and watch the show on the Square; or you can sit back and watch the setting sun put on its show. Either way, Glen's Peppermint Soda is a tingling, refreshing late afternoon drink.

1½ ounces vodka	*club soda*
½ ounce peppermint schnapps	*1 sprig of mint*

Fill a 12-ounce glass with ice and pour in the vodka and schnapps. Fill the glass to the top with club soda and garnish with a sprig of mint.

1 serving.

Nuts and Berries

Ellen Rochford, from The Top at La Concha in Key West, won first prize in Key West and second prize in Florida for this hazelnut-flavored drink. She serves it in a long-stemmed tulip glass and garnishes it with a small scoop of ice cream, a hazelnut, and a raspberry.

½ cup vanilla ice cream	*3 lime leaves*
1 ounce Frangelico liqueur	*1 hazelnut*
½ ounce Chambord raspberry liqueur	*1 fresh raspberry*
1 small scoop vanilla ice cream	

Place ½ cup ice cream in a blender container and add the liqueurs. Blend. Pour into tulip glass and garnish with a small scoop of ice cream. Stand the lime leaves upright together in the ice cream and put the hazelnut and raspberry in the center of the leaves.

1 serving.

Duval Crawl

What do you do when it's cloudy or rainy and you can't go to the beach? In Key West, everyone crawls up and down Duval Street, window shopping, eating, and drinking. Bruce Cernicky, manager of the Hyatt Key West's Nick's Upstairs Bar and Restaurant, serves this drink to cheer everyone up. It's a six-liquor drink served in a 22-ounce glass. The tropical-drink menu at Nick's is one of the most extensive I've seen and gives a complete explanation of every drink.

The drink is served in a super thistle glass, which can be found in a restaurant supply store. A large tulip glass will also work.

¼ ounce vodka
¼ ounce gin
¼ ounce white rum
¼ ounce peach liqueur
¼ ounce amaretto liqueur
¼ ounce blue curaçao

½ cup unsweetened pineapple juice
splash of 7 Up
2 maraschino cherries
½ slice lemon
½ slice lime

Fill a blender container ¾ full with ice. Add the liquid ingredients and blend until smooth. Pour into a 22-ounce glass and garnish with the cherries and the lemon and lime slices.

1 to 6 servings, depending on your thirst.

Lion's Paw Grog

Thirsty sailors on the Alvarez yacht, the *Lion's Paw,* dip into the bucket hanging from the boom after a day of racing and enjoy this fruit-and-rum drink. Ripe, fresh fruit is the key. Debbie and Rick Alvarez make this drink in a 2½-gallon stainless steel bucket, place a ladle inside, and hang it up for everyone to help themselves. Their recipe is for 20 people, but I have provided quantities to serve 6. Simply quadruple the amounts if you're having a large party. The Alvarezes say this is for enjoyment only while at anchor.

1½ cups banana nectar	*2 limes, sliced*
1½ cups mango nectar	*1 kiwi, peeled and sliced*
1½ cups fresh orange juice	*1 banana, peeled and sliced*
1½ cups dark rum	*1 orange, sliced and seeds removed*
½ pound strawberries, washed, hulled, and quartered	*1 apple, cored and sliced*
	¼ cup grated coconut
¼ pound seedless grapes	

Combine the ingredients in a bowl or large pitcher and let sit 30 minutes. Ladle into ice-filled glasses.

6 servings.

Key West Sunset

The Casa Marina sits at the end of the road overlooking the Atlantic in Key West. It opened on New Year's Eve in 1922 and has had a checkered past, housing the Navy in 1943 and the Army during the Cuban missile crisis in 1962. The Marriott chain took it over in 1978 and it has regained hotel status once more. The beautiful lawns lead down to an 1,100-foot beach and a perfect Keys sunset. The Calabesh Lounge serves this drink to mimic the colors of the setting sun.

*1¼ ounces Cuervo Gold tequila
orange juice
splash of grenadine*

*1 slice of orange
1 maraschino cherry*

Fill a 12-ounce glass with ice and pour in the tequila. Fill the glass with orange juice and add a splash of grenadine. Garnish with a slice of orange and a maraschino cherry.

1 serving.

Kokomo

Michael, at the Roof Top Café in Key West, won the Malibu award for this drink that tastes something like a creamsicle.

*1 ounce Nassau royale liqueur
  (vanilla-flavored liqueur)
1 ounce Malibu coconut rum
⅓ cup Coco Lopez cream of coconut*

*1 ounce Key lime juice
1 orange, juiced (about ¼ cup)
2 cups ice*

Place the ingredients in a blender container and blend until thick.

1 serving.

Kokomotion

For this coconut drink, Steve, from the Roof Top Café, won first prize in Key West at the Myers's Rum contest. Although cream of coconut is used as a base, the Key lime juice makes it less sweet than other frozen drinks.

¼ cup Coco Lopez cream of coconut
¼ cup Key lime juice

1¼ ounces Myers's rum

Fill a blender container with ice one-quarter full. Add the cream of coconut and Key lime juice and blend until smooth. Pour the rum into an 8-ounce glass and pour the blended mixture on top.

1 serving.

Ocean Blue Margarita

Stop at The Top in the La Concha Hotel on Duval Street in Key West to see a panoramic view of the entire city. Ellen Rochford created her award-winning drink to match the art deco colors that impressed her when she came to Florida. This drink is turquoise-blue and is garnished with a pink coral hibiscus. It's served in a wide-rimmed margarita glass.

1 ounce Cuervo Gold tequila
½ ounce Cointreau
1 ounce blue curaçao
1 ounce sweet-and-sour mix
   (Mr. and Mrs. T's)

½ ounce Rose's Lime Juice, plus enough to wet
   glasses
salt
slice of lime
halved hibiscus flowers

Fill a blender container three-quarters full with ice. Pour in the tequila, Cointreau, curaçao, sweet-and-sour mix, and ½ ounce Rose's Lime Juice and blend. Wet the rims of 2 glasses with the additional Rose's Lime Juice and dip them into salt. Pour the contents of the blender into the glasses. Garnish each with a half slice of lime and a hibiscus flower.

2 servings.

Sally's Calamondin Liqueur

Australians named this fruit, which is shaped like a very small tangerine. Calamondins are highly acidic, which makes them perfect for marmalades or beverages. Sally Thomas's calamondin tree in her yard in Key West is so prolific that she can make enough liqueur to share with her lucky friends.

40 to 50 calamondins
1 cup sugar

3 cups vodka

Wash and chop calamondins and mix with the sugar in a large jar. Pour in the vodka and leave the jar in a dark cupboard for at least forty days, turning the jar over every ten days or so. I left it for four months, and the perfumed vodka was an ambrosia. Strain through cheesecloth and bottle ready for use.

1 pint liqueur.

SOUPS

The abundance of fresh fish in the Keys makes chowders and fish soups a natural in Keys cooking. Soups capture and blend the flavors of their fresh ingredients. They are an inviting start to a meal and a measure of the quality of the chef. Traditional conch chowder made with a spicy tomato base is served in most restaurants. Using lots of conch, fresh vegetables, and a touch of sherry, Ziggie's Conch Chowder is a recipe worth trying. Marker 88 Conch Bisque is a tasty, unique cream-based conch chowder.

The secret to a good fish chowder is the quality of the fish used. If you can't find the fish called for in these recipes, then use the best and freshest white-fleshed fish available to you; stay away from dark-fleshed oily fish such as mackerel or salmon when making soup.

Black Bean Soup is as representative of Keys cooking as any dish. André Mueller adds his European touch to this Cuban staple to create a flavor that his Cuban friends love.

Cold soups on hot nights are as refreshing as hot soups are satisfying on cold nights. Papaya and Orange Soup is an unusual, palate-pleasing blend of flavors, while Shrimp Gazpacho adds a tropical twist to this dish of Spanish origin.

Many of these soups are a meal in themselves. To enjoy a light Keys supper, serve these soups with some good crusty bread and beer or a cool glass of chablis.

Soups

Ziggie's Conch Chowder 57

Bec's Grouper Chowder 58

Conch Bisque 59

Green Turtle Inn Turtle Consommé 60

Chilled Papaya and Orange Soup 61

Snook's Bayside Club Bouillabaisse 62

Marker 88 Black Bean Soup 63

B's Garbanzo Soup 64

Shrimp Gazpacho 66

Ziggie's Conch Chowder

Conch Chowder appears everywhere in the Keys. This is an especially good recipe. Henri Champagne has been making it at Ziggie's for years.

1 pound conch*
½ pound bacon or salt pork, diced
1 clove garlic, crushed
3 quarts water
2 cups clam juice
4 tomatoes, quartered
2 carrots, peeled and diced
1 large onion, diced

1 stalk celery, diced
2 large potatoes, peeled and cut into ½-inch
  chunks
1 cup tomato juice
1 tablespoon dried thyme
4 or 5 drops Tabasco sauce
salt and freshly ground white pepper
½ cup dry sherry

Rinse the conch, cut off the orange fin and the foot and discard. Finely dice the conch, or coarsely chop in food processor. Sauté the bacon and garlic. Add conch and sauté 30 seconds. Add the water and bring to a boil. Simmer, covered, 20 minutes. Add the clam juice, tomatoes, carrots, onion, and celery. When the liquid comes back to a boil, add the potatoes, tomato juice, thyme, and Tabasco. Simmer, uncovered, for 20 to 25 minutes. Add salt and pepper to taste. Just before serving, add the sherry. The sherry should just sit in the hot soup.

8 servings.

*Substitute any edible whelk, clams, or abalone for the conch.

Bec's Grouper Chowder

Sis Kelm has been a Keys resident for twenty years. Her husband, Erv, goes fishing every Monday. Every Tuesday her friends line up at noon, pots in hand, hoping for some of her fish chowder. Bec, Sis's housekeeper of forty-two years, developed this recipe for her, and she's been making it for years.

Hog snapper or other firm white-fleshed fish may be used instead of grouper. Oily fish such as mackerel or bluefish are not suitable.

2 8-ounce bottles clam juice	1 teaspoon sugar
3 pounds grouper	1 teaspoon salt
1 pound salt pork or bacon, cubed (optional)	½ teaspoon white pepper
3 large onions, sliced	2 tablespoons butter
2 large potatoes, peeled and cubed	1 quart half-and-half
1½ cups diced celery	1 12-ounce can evaporated milk
2 bay leaves	¼ teaspoon paprika

Pour the clam juice into a large pan and bring to a simmer. Place the grouper in the liquid, bring to a simmer, cover, and poach for 15 minutes; do not let the liquid boil or the fish will be tough. Remove the fish to a plate and reserve the stock. Sauté the pork in a heavy skillet until golden and crisp. Drain on paper towels. Add the onions to the drippings and gently sauté until golden. Drain on paper towels.

Place the onions, potatoes, celery, bay leaves, sugar, salt, and pepper in a large pot. Measure the poaching liquid and add water to make 2 cups. Add to the pot with the butter. Bring to a boil, reduce heat, cover, and simmer 15 minutes. In a separate saucepan or microwave oven, heat the half-and-half until tepid; pour into the pot. Add the evaporated milk and taste for seasoning. Do not let the liquid boil once the cream and milk have been added.

Break the poached fish into 1-inch pieces and stir into the hot soup. Remove from heat and allow to set to develop flavor. Remove bay leaves. Gently reheat. Sprinkle pork cubes and paprika on top and serve.

8 to 10 servings.

Conch Bisque

This bisque recipe from Marker 88 varies from the tomato-based conch chowder that has become synonymous with cooking in the Keys. It's a cream-based, or white, soup, as opposed to the usual red one. If conch is unavailable, any edible whelk, clams, or abalone may be substituted.

¾ *pound conch*
2 quarts cold water
2 teaspoons salt
1 bouquet garni (made with 1 stalk celery, 1 leek, 3 or 4 sprigs fresh parsley, 2-inch piece fresh ginger, quartered lengthwise, tied together with string)

2 tablespoons butter
¼ *cup flour*
½ *cup heavy cream*
¼ *cup dry sherry*

Rinse the conch, cut off the orange fin and the foot and discard. This will make it easier to grind. Grind the conch in a meat grinder or chop using a food processor. Place in a large pot with the cold water, salt, and bouquet garni. Bring the water to a boil and simmer for 1½ hours. Strain the soup, reserving the broth. Set the conch meat aside and discard the bouquet garni.

Melt the butter in a second saucepan. Stir in the flour to form a loose paste. Add the strained soup, a little at a time, stirring constantly with a whisk. Return the conch meat to the soup. Bring to a boil, reduce heat, and simmer for 15 minutes. Add the heavy cream and heat just to simmering. Either add the sherry just before serving or serve it on the side to be added according to taste.

6 servings, 1¼ quarts of soup.

Green Turtle Inn Turtle Consommé

Roxie and Sid Siderius opened the Green Turtle Inn in 1947 and it quickly became a favorite of the locals. At one time it was one of the only restaurants in the Upper Keys. Its old frame building is one of the few that survived the catastrophic 1935 hurricane. The decor hasn't changed much. The pictures covering the walls depict the Keys of the late forties and fifties.

At that time green turtle was a staple food in the Keys and at the Inn. With a lack of refrigeration and fresh meat, people lived on what they could catch. The green turtles weighing 250 to 300 pounds were high in protein and good to eat. Large turtle steaks were marinated in oil, paprika, and Key lime juice and then grilled. In 1978, the United States banned the use of green turtle meat in order to protect this rapidly diminishing species. You can still see the Turtle Krals in Key West where the turtles were brought in from the Grand Cayman Islands and kept in water-filled paddocks until they were needed. Today, the Green Turtle Inn consommé is made with fresh-water turtle. This turtle is not large enough to be cut into steaks, so its use is limited to making soup and chowder.

Henry Rosenthal took over the Green Turtle Inn in the mid seventies and has been running it and its companion cannery ever since. Under the original Sid and Roxie label, Henry has been selling his turtle consommé, turtle chowder, and Key lime pie filling.

I tried this recipe, substituting chicken for the turtle, and the result was a delicious consommé.

4 pounds turtle meat or chicken parts, cut into chunks	8 envelopes unflavored gelatin
4 quarts water	1 teaspoon salt
4 cups carrots, peeled and roughly chopped	½ cup Maggi liquid seasoning
4 cups onions, roughly chopped	2 cups cooked rice (1 cup uncooked)
4 bay leaves	1 cup chopped fresh parsley
	½ cup sherry

Place the turtle meat in the water with the carrots and onions tied in a piece of cheesecloth. Add the bay leaves, gelatin, salt, and liquid seasoning. Bring the water to a boil, and reduce heat to a simmer. Cover and simmer 5 to 6 hours or overnight. Remove the cheesecloth bag and correct the seasoning. Serve hot or at room temperature. Serve each portion with rice and a garnish of parsley. Add a spoonful of sherry to each serving or leave the sherry on the table for everyone to help him- or herself, as they do at the Inn.

6 to 8 servings.

Chilled Papaya and Orange Soup

Nick's Upstairs at the Hyatt Key West overlooks the courtyard and ocean beyond. It's a beautiful setting for this very tropical soup. The soup is served in a giant martini glass and is also used as a sauce for shrimp. The recipe makes one serving, which is how the restaurant makes and serves this soup. You can increase the quantities to prepare for a larger number.

½ small ripe papaya, seeded and peeled	3 tablespoons powdered sugar
¼ cup orange juice	2 endive leaves
1 tablespoon kirsch	1 slice kiwi

Puree the papaya in the container of a blender or food processor. Add the orange juice, kirsch, and powdered sugar. Add more juice if the mixture is too thick, and more sugar if not sweet enough. Pour the soup into a bowl and stand the endive leaves together on the side. Float the kiwi slice near the leaves.

1 serving.

Snook's Bayside Club Bouillabaisse

Lounging on the deck at Snook's, the sea surrounds you and the sunlight reflects brilliantly off the water. Pat Mathias, chef and part owner, takes treasures from the sea, including yellowtail caught by her husband, to make this Keys fish stew. With some bread and a salad, it is a meal in itself. The secret to this dish is the sweet fresh fish, good olive oil, and butter. This recipe makes one serving, and that is how the restaurant makes and serves this soup. You can increase the quantities to prepare for a larger number, but be careful to cook the fish and seafood individually to maintain their quality.

¼ cup Mild Fish Stock (recipe follows) or water
¼ cup white wine
3 tablespoons olive oil
3 tablespoons unsalted butter
½ tomato, peeled and chopped
1 tablespoon chopped shallot
1 small clove garlic, crushed
1 sprig fresh thyme
½ Florida lobster tail in shell

2 clams
2 to 3 ounces yellowtail fillet
4 sea scallops
3 shrimp
2 mussels
pinch of saffron
1 stone crab claw (in season)
salt and white pepper to taste
1 tablespoon chopped fresh parsley

Prepare the Mild Fish Stock. Place ¼ cup stock and the white wine, oil, butter, tomato, shallot, garlic, and thyme in a saucepan and bring to a simmer. Cut the half lobster tail in half again and place in the liquid, meat-side down. Simmer, covered, 1 minute. Add the clams and then the yellowtail; simmer 1 minute. Add the scallops, shrimp, and mussels and simmer 2 more minutes. Dissolve the saffron in 1 tablespoon hot water and add to the saucepan. Add crab claw at end and cook just long enough to take the chill off. Transfer the seafood to a serving bowl. If any of the fish is not yet cooked, return it to the liquid for another minute. Remove the clams from their shells and place on half shells in the serving bowl. Taste the liquid for seasoning, adding salt and pepper as necessary. Pour the liquid over the seafood. Serve sprinkled with chopped parsley.

1 serving.

◆
Mild Fish Stock

1 yellowtail head	½ cup water
½ small fennel bulb, sliced	½ cup white wine

Combine the ingredients in saucepan and simmer for 1 hour. Strain and reserve for use.
Makes 1 cup stock.

Marker 88 Black Bean Soup

André Mueller combines his European background with the Cuban foods he has learned to love since coming to the Keys. He uses kielbasa sausage because it gives a light flavor and chuckles when his Cuban friends ask him about the secret ingredient in their favorite soup.

2 cups dried black beans	1 teaspoon salt
1 cup diced kielbasa	1 teaspoon freshly ground black pepper
1 cup diced onion	1 teaspoon Maggi liquid seasoning
1 cup diced green pepper	1 cup diced onion
2 quarts water	4 cups cooked white rice (2 cups uncooked)
6 bay leaves	

Soak the beans in enough water to cover for at least 8 hours or overnight. Drain. Sauté the kielbasa in a large pot. No fat is needed; the sausage will give off enough of its own. Add the onion and green pepper and simmer until softened. Add the black beans, water, bay leaves, salt, pepper, and Maggi liquid seasoning. Bring to a boil and simmer for about 2 hours or until the beans are soft.

Serve the soup topped with diced onions and with a bowl of rice on the side. Spoon some rice into each bowl as the soup is served.

8 to 10 servings.

B's Garbanzo Soup

B's Restaurant on Bertha Street in Key West is popular among the locals for Cuban food. Sitting at the bar, I asked one of the regulars what his B's favorite was. "Garbanzo soup," was his immediate answer. Bertha Mira, who helps run her family's restaurant, says that they make a different fresh soup everyday except Wednesdays and Saturdays, when by popular demand they make their Garbanzo Soup. After tasting it, I understood why.

Flank or skirt steak is used in this recipe for flavor only. After the steak is cooked it is removed and used to make Ropa Vieja, a well-known Cuban favorite. Ropa Vieja means "old clothes" and is made with flank steak that has been cooked and then shredded. Vegetables and tomato sauce make up the balance of the recipe. Bertha tells me that using the meat for two dishes is very common and the best way to make the most out of available food.

Sofrito is a basic Spanish sauce used to add depth of flavor in many Cuban recipes. It usually contains onions, garlic, green pepper, tomatoes, spices, and sometimes ham. All of the ingredients are cooked in oil. In this recipe the sofrito is made with onions, garlic, and pepper.

Bijol is a Latin spice made from ground annatto seed. It gives the food a yellow color much the same way saffron does. Tumeric may be used instead.

1 pound garbanzos (chick-peas), rinsed
4 quarts salted water
1 pound flank steak
1 ham hock or 1½ pounds boneless ham
3 tablespoons olive oil
1 large onion, sliced
½ head garlic, peeled and crushed

1 green pepper, sliced
2 pounds potatoes, peeled and cubed
1 pound chorizo sausage, thickly sliced
2 cups thickly sliced cabbage
1 teaspoon bijol or tumeric
salt and freshly ground black pepper to taste

Soak the garbanzos in a large pot of salted water overnight. Cut the flank steak into four pieces and add to the beans with the ham hock. Make sure the ingredients are well covered with water; you don't want to have to add water later and dilute the flavor. Boil until the beans begin to soften, about 30 minutes.

Meanwhile make the sofrito. Heat the oil in a skillet and add the onion, garlic, and green pepper. Fry until soft. When the beans start to soften, remove the flank steak and save for other use. Scrape the ham off the bone and return the ham bits to the soup. Add the potatoes, sofrito, chorizos, and cabbage and continue to cook until the potatoes and beans are soft, about 45 minutes. Add the bijol and cook 5 more minutes. Taste for seasoning, adding salt and pepper as necessary.

8 to 10 servings, 2 to 3 quarts soup.

Shrimp Gazpacho

La Te Da's charm is its slightly seedy yet elegant decor. It's been in Key West for a long time and has become a fixture there. This cold soup was perfect for a warm Sunday's brunch while sitting around their pool. It whips up in seconds. If you're really in a hurry, you can buy cooked shrimp instead of boiling your own.

3 cups V-8 juice
3 cups tomato juice
½ cup red wine vinegar
½ yellow pepper, diced
½ red pepper, diced
1 cucumber, peeled, seeded, and diced
1 stalk celery, diced
½ medium onion, diced

2 teaspoons fresh tarragon or 1 teaspoon dried
*   tarragon*
4 drops Tabasco sauce
salt and freshly ground black pepper to taste
12 cooked shrimp, peeled and cut in half
*   lengthwise (see Carriage Trade Garden Key*
*   West Shrimp, page 13)*

Combine the ingredients, except the shrimp, in a large bowl. Taste for seasoning, adding more Tabasco, salt, or pepper as needed. Serve in individual bowls and float 4 shrimp slices in each bowl.

6 servings.

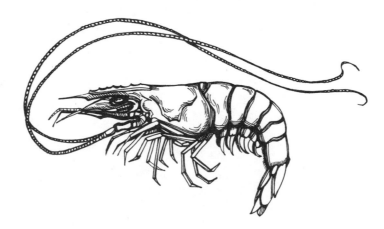

MAIN COURSES

A book on cooking in the Keys must concentrate on fish and shellfish. Conch, stone crabs, blue crabs, shrimp, and Florida lobster are on nearly every menu along with yellowtail, grouper, dolphin, and pompano.

Names such as bonefish and permit have been prominent in the news since President Bush's fishing trips to the Keys. Bonefish are game fish and not usually used for table food, while a 6- to 8-pound permit can be very similar to pompano.

The Florida Keys provide one of the best sport-fishing areas in the world, and local restaurants have access to these fresh and unusual species. Chefs who have worked in various parts of the world have commented on the extraordinary texture, flavor, and freshness of Keys fish. The dishes are wonderful because the fish is so fresh. So, when buying your fish, make sure you choose the very freshest fish available to you and substitute it in the recipes.

Knowing how to cook fish is as important as knowing how to buy it. The section entitled Hints on Cooking Fish is provided to assist you in preparing these and your own fish recipes.

The Cuban influence enhances the recipes in this section. These ethnic dishes use cinnamon, cumin, bijol, cloves, and sour orange to create exciting taste combinations. Cuban roast pork, arroz con pollo, bolichi, and picadillo are all traditional dishes and very much a part of Keys cuisine. A new type of cuisine, based on Latin cooking, is now being developed by chefs who are combining the various influences present in the Keys. Black beans are made into a spicy relish; tropical fruits are used with meat sauces; chorizo sausages are grilled with shrimp; and plantains are sautéed with cinnamon.

Usually, either fried or baked potatoes and a salad accompany the main course. More recently, some tropical vegetables such as boniato, chayote squash, and malanga are becoming popular. Try these unusual accompaniments to complete your menus.

Shellfish and Fish Main Courses

Ziggie's Cracked Conch 79

André's Cracked Conch and Garlic Butter 80

Eddie Wightman's Grilled Crawfish 82

Manny and Isa's Fried Lobster 83

Manny and Isa's Lobster Enchilado 84

Dorothy Hertel's Seafood Linguine 85

Steamed Blue Crabs 87

Tugboat Crab Cakes with Tartar Sauce 88

Ziggie's Stone Crabs with Mustard Sauce 89

Craig's Shrimp Scampi 90

Spicy Shrimp with Mango, Avocado, and Chardonnay—Louie's
Backyard 91

Key West Shrimp Boil with Key Lime Mustard Sauce 94

Seafood Collin 95

HINTS ON COOKING FISH

Obtaining absolutely fresh fish is half the secret to enjoying it. The rest is in its preparation. Overcooking will leave the best fish dry and tasteless. So, here are some hints on how to cook fish.

Grilling

Grilling is a popular Keys method of cooking fish. When you've come back from a long day of fishing, it's very satisfying to light the grill and cook outside while the sun sets. Most fish and shellfish can be grilled.

Whole fish or firm-textured fish cut into steaks is best for grilling. Fillets tend to fall apart when moved or turned on the grill. If you are grilling fillets, then make sure the skin is left on and start them on the grill skin side down. If you have a grill with a hood you can avoid having to turn the fish over by searing one side, moving it to the edge where the heat is less intense, and lowering the lid. If a whole fish is quite thick, make a couple of diagonal slashes across the body on both sides so that the heat will penetrate better. Make sure your grilling grates are clean and brush them with some vegetable oil to help prevent sticking. You can buy special grates with handles that are shaped to hold fish. Again, if you use these, be sure to oil them first.

To avoid overcooking whole fish and steaks, place the fish in the center of the grill to sear it. Turn it to sear the second side and then move it to the edge of the grill where the heat is lower. A general rule of thumb is to cook the fish for ten minutes for each inch of thickness measured at the thickest part of the fish.

To test for doneness, stick the point of a knife into the thickest section and gently pull some of the meat away. The flesh should be opaque, but juicy. Remember, the fish will continue to cook for a few minutes after it is removed from the heat.

Poaching

Cooking fish in a court bouillon, a water and white wine bath, helps to preserve moisture and is an excellent method of cooking fish that will be served cold or at room temperature. The fish should be placed on a rack and gently lowered into the hot liquid. The liquid should just cover the fish and should be brought only to a simmer. Never let the liquid boil; it will make the fish rubbery. If you are going to serve the fish cold, then undercook it and remove the pan from the heat. Let the fish cool in the liquid and it will remain juicy and tender.

A general rule is to poach fish for 10 minutes per pound. I prefer to cook it 7 to 8 minutes and then check to see if it is done. Remember, as in grilling, the fish will continue to cook after it is removed from the heat.

Baking

Fish should be baked at 450 degrees. The high heat will seal in the juices. Fatty fish, such as bluefish and mackerel, do not need extra fat, while leaner fish will need some butter or oil. Usually fish is baked in a pan with chopped carrots, onion, celery, and some water and white wine. Many Keys recipes call for baking the fish in a tomato sauce.

The general rule is to cover the pan with foil and to bake the fish at 450 degrees for about 10 minutes per pound. Check the fish after 7 minutes to make sure it doesn't overcook.

Broiling

Be sure to preheat your broiler. I place a baking sheet or pan in to preheat as well. This way the radiant heat from the pan will cook the fish on the bottom and it will not need turning. Always brush the fish with oil to protect it and place it about 3 to 4 inches from the heat.

Broil fish for about 8 minutes per inch of thickness. Measure the fish at its thickest point.

Frying

Frying is very popular in the Keys. It seals in the juices and creates a tasty outer coating. Be sure you have fresh, clean frying oil. I prefer to fry fish at between 350 and 375 degrees. If the oil is not hot enough, the fish will absorb it and become heavy. If the oil is too hot, the outer coating will burn and the inside won't be done. Fry just a few pieces at a time so that they won't stick together and you'll be able to monitor their progress. Serve fried fish immediately. If left to sit, the steam that is trapped inside, keeping the fish moist, will escape, making the crust soggy.

A piece of fish 1 to 2 inches thick will fry in 2 to 3 minutes. Larger pieces will take only a few minutes longer.

Oven Steaming

Wrapping the fish with vegetables in foil and letting it cook in its own juices is an excellent method of cooking fish. Fresh herbs, wine, or cheese may be added. The natural juices, plus any added liquid, will make a delicious sauce and when you open the packet the aroma will be wonderful.

In general, I like to oven-steam fish at 450 degrees. It should take about 10 minutes for a 1-inch fillet.

Sautéing

This method is best for fillets or flatfish. Make sure you use a heavy-bottomed pan so that the heat is evenly distributed. Melt the butter or oil so that it covers the bottom of the pan and do not use a lid. Sauté the fish until it is a golden color on both sides.

CONCH

Conch, pronounced "konk," is a spiral-shaped gastropod. It lives in a large spiral shell and can be very tough. It needs to be tenderized before use. It can also be eaten raw. One Keys friend tells me that he used to go out fishing with his grandparents and take all of the fixings for a conch salad along. They would catch the conch and eat it right there on the boat. Today, because they have been overfished, it is illegal to fish for conch off the United States coast. As a result, we now get our conch imported and frozen. Those of you on the West Coast will find that the recipes work well with abalone substituted for the conch.

To Tenderize Conch

There are several schools as to whether or not conch should be tenderized. I have eaten raw or marinated conch and it was beautifully tender. I have also eaten it cooked and couldn't chew it at all. Much depends on the quality and freshness of the conch. To be on the safe side ask the fish man to tenderize the conch for you. He passes it through a machine that does the job in seconds. If tenderizing it at home, first cut off the orange fin and the foot. Then slice the conch in half lengthwise to make it thinner. You can use a meat mallet or the bottom of a bottle pounding diagonally in one direction and then again in the opposite direction.

Conch, Nickname of Natives

Conch is a term used to describe the British who lived in Key West at the time of the Revolutionary War and didn't want to fight England. They fled to English possessions, such as the Grand Bahamas, during the Revolution and drifted back to Key West by the 1830's.

They were sea folk and conch was their staple food. The shell was used as a horn and as a symbol on their clan standards. Natives of long standing adopt the name, but this angers the descendants of the so-called real conchs.

One legend holds that in the days of buccaneers unknown ships would hoist a friendly conch shell to their foremast to gain entry to a port. More often than not, they entered the harbor, raised the Jolly Roger, and sacked the settlement.

The Conch Republic

On April 18, 1982, the United States Border Patrol set up a road block in Florida to prohibit illegal aliens from entering the country. The Keys were treated as a foreign land and people entering or leaving had to prove United States citizenship. On April 23, 1982, in mock protest, Key West declared its independence from the United States and called itself The Conch Republic.

Ziggie's Cracked Conch

The Conch has been an institution in the Upper Keys since 1966, when it was opened by Ziggie (Sigmund) Stocki, a well-known chef who had been cooking in the Keys since 1952. After Ziggie died, his wife, Virginia Stocki, took over the restaurant and runs it with her son, Alan. Henri Champagne, their chef, has been with them since 1966 turning out delicious Keys food.

The restaurant has linoleum floors, Formica-topped tables, and paper place mats. Wear your sandals and shorts and enjoy the local atmosphere and food.

1½ pounds conch, tenderized
3 tablespoons lemon juice
3 tablespoons Worcestershire sauce
1 teaspoon salt
2 teaspoons white pepper
1½ cups all-purpose flour

1½ tablespoons baking powder
½ teaspoon salt
¾ cup beer
*1 cup mango chutney (any mango chutney is
  fine)*

Ask the fish man to tenderize the conch for you. If tenderizing yourself, rinse the conch, cut off the orange fin and the foot and discard. Then slice the conch in half lengthwise to make it thinner. You can use a meat mallet or the bottom of a bottle pounding diagonally in one direction and then again in the opposite direction. In a large bowl combine the lemon juice, Worcestershire, salt, and pepper. In a second bowl, combine the flour, baking powder, and salt. Add just enough beer to moisten the flour. Soak the conch in the sauce for a few minutes and then dip in the batter. Make sure you have a thin coating of batter, scraping off some if necessary. Heat the oil to 350 degrees, place the conch in a basket, and slowly lower it into the oil. Shake the basket to keep the conch from sticking. Fry 2 to 3 minutes until golden and crispy. Serve with mango chutney.

6 servings.

André's Cracked Conch and Garlic Butter

When André Mueller of Marker 88 restaurant arrived in the Keys in the 1960's, deep-fried foods in heavy batter were prevalent. He wanted a fish with a light batter that was gently sautéed. His cracked conch recipe has been imitated throughout the Keys. It's modern, it's light, and it's delicious.

2 pounds conch, tenderized
2 tablespoons lime juice
1 tablespoon Worcestershire sauce
2 eggs
2 tablespoons milk

2 tablespoons oil
flour for coating
2 tablespoons clarified butter (see Glossary) or
   1 tablespoon each butter and oil

Ask the fish man to tenderize the conch for you. If tenderizing yourself, rinse the conch, cut off the orange fin and the foot and discard. Then slice the conch in half lengthwise to make it thinner. You can use a meat mallet or the bottom of a bottle pounding diagonally in one direction and then again in the opposite direction. Mix the lime juice and Worcestershire in a bowl. In a second bowl mix the egg, milk, and oil to form an egg wash. Place the flour in a third bowl. Dip the conch in lime juice and then in flour, shaking the excess off; there should be only a very thin coat of flour on the conch. Dip the conch in egg wash. Heat the butter in a skillet and sauté the conch for 2 minutes. Turn and sauté another 2 minutes. Don't overcook conch. Place on warm serving dish and cover with foil while you prepare garlic butter. Serve with garlic butter either spooned over the conch or on the side for dipping.

4 servings.

♦

Garlic Butter

½ cup butter (1 stick)
1 tablespoon crushed garlic
2 teaspoons chopped fresh parsley
¼ teaspoon chopped shallot

1 tablespoon white wine
1 teaspoon lemon juice
¼ teaspoon white pepper

Partially melt the butter in a saucepan over low heat; it should still be thick. Briskly whip in the garlic, parsley, and shallot. Refrigerate; the butter should be cold for the next step. When ready to use, remove from refrigerator and over low heat whip in the white wine and lemon juice. If the heat is too high, the butter will break down and separate. Add pepper to taste. Serve immediately.

Makes about ½ cup sauce.

FLORIDA LOBSTER

Florida lobster is also called a spiny lobster or spiny crawfish. This shellfish is easily recognized by the prominent spines on its body and five pairs of legs. Unlike the Maine lobster, it does not have claws. The body is discarded and the large tail that provides the meat can be boiled, broiled, steamed, deep-fried, or grilled. The lobster season is controlled and runs from August 6th to March 31st. Lobster tails are sold frozen all over the United States and will work well in these recipes.

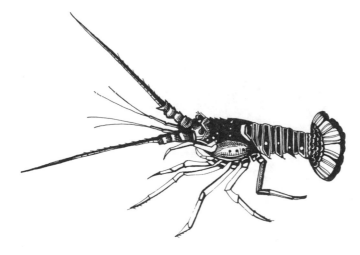

Eddie Wightman's Grilled Crawfish

Eddie Wightman is a well-known backcountry fishing guide. His recipe for grilled crawfish has become very popular among his fellow fishermen.

6 spiny crawfish
¼ cup sherry
1 cup butter (2 sticks)

1 clove garlic, crushed
1 lemon, juiced

Light the grill and let the coals burn down. Separate the tail from the body of the crawfish; discard the body. Split the hard side of the tail with a sharp knife or poultry shears. Butterfly the fish in its shell by slitting the meat in half lengthwise, cutting to the other shell, but not through it. Spread out the shell. Prepare each of the crawfish in this manner. Sprinkle the meat with sherry. Melt the butter with the garlic. Brush the meat with the butter mixture and sprinkle with lemon juice. Place on the grill with the meat side up. This recipe works best if the grill is covered. The lobster will cook through evenly without the bottom drying out. If you have an open grill, place a piece of foil loosely over the crawfish to trap the heat. Grill until the meat is opaque, about 10 minutes. Serve immediately.

6 servings.

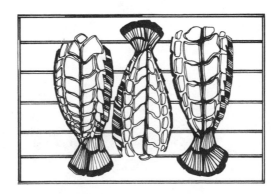

Manny and Isa's Fried Lobster

Lightly frying lobster seals in the juices and brings out its sweet flavor. This same recipe can be used for frying shrimp, Maine lobster meat, or monk fish.

4 Florida lobster tails
2 tablespoons lime juice
4 cloves garlic, crushed
1 teaspoon salt
1 teaspoon white pepper
½ cup milk
1 egg

½ cup all-purpose flour
1 cup fine cracker meal
3 to 4 cups oil for frying (depending on size of pot)
4 or 5 washed lettuce leaves
4 tablespoons chopped fresh parsley
½ cup butter (1 stick), melted

Ask the fish store to cut the lobster in half for you. Remove the tail meat from the shell. Slit the meat open. Sprinkle with lime juice and rub with a little garlic, salt, and pepper. Whisk the milk and egg together. Dip each tail in the egg mixture and then roll in flour. Dip in the egg mixture again and roll in cracker meal. Heat oil to 365 degrees and fry the lobster tails for 5 to 10 minutes, adding one tail at a time to the oil. As the oil comes back to temperature, add the next tail until all are cooked.

Serve each lobster tail on lettuce and sprinkle with parsley. Pour the melted butter into small individual bowls and place on each lobster plate for dipping.

4 servings.

Manny and Isa's Lobster Enchilado

Manny and Isa developed this recipe with memories of the enchilados of their native Cuba. They took the Florida lobster and shrimp and cooked it in their own familiar tomato sauce.

Enchilado means red sauce and looks like the Mexican word *enchilada*, but their meanings are different.

2 15-ounce cans tomato sauce	*2 teaspoons ground cumin*
2 cups diced onions	*½ teaspoon oregano*
2 green peppers, diced	*½ teaspoon freshly ground black pepper*
2 whole red pimentos, diced	*4 Florida lobsters or 24 large shrimp*
2 cloves garlic, crushed	*6 sprigs fresh parsley*

Place the ingredients, except the lobsters and parsley, in a large saucepan, cover, and simmer for 20 minutes. Taste for seasoning, adding more pepper, cumin, or oregano, if necessary.

Remove the lobster meat from each tail and cut into bite-size pieces. Simmer in the tomato sauce for 10 to 15 minutes. Alternatively, shell and devein the shrimp. Make a slit down the back of the shrimp lengthwise and remove the black vein. Rinse and cook in the tomato sauce for 10–15 minutes. Do not boil or overcook or the meat will be rubbery. Serve with white rice and garnish with parsley.

4 servings.

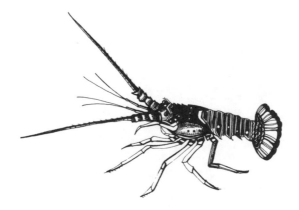

Dorothy Hertel's Seafood Linguine

"I love Islamorada and wouldn't move anywhere else. It is what small town America used to be. Everyone knows everyone else and they all help each other," says Dorothy Hertel about this idyllic spot where she has made her home. When Gary Ellis started the Redbone Celebrity Tournament in 1988, the entire community supported him. It has become a part of the autumn Islamorada schedule, raising tens of thousands of dollars for cystic fibrosis. This is the type of community involvement and concern that make Islamorada a special place for the Hertels.

The laid-back atmosphere and the beckoning sea brought Dorothy to Islamorada in 1984 from Davie, Florida. She bought the Islamorada Fish Company and learned the business quickly. She and her husband and partner, George, bring in the best and freshest fish possible. They carry local fish, with Florida lobster and stone crabs their specialty, and only import fish on special request.

As would be expected, Dorothy and George love fish, and this is one of their favorite recipes.

1 tablespoon olive oil	1 48-ounce jar tomato sauce
1 green pepper, sliced	½ teaspoon fresh thyme or ¼ teaspoon dried
1 red pepper, sliced	2 tablespoons freshly ground black pepper
8 ounces mushrooms, washed and sliced	4 tablespoons sour cream
2 cloves garlic, crushed	2 tablespoons Dat'l Do-it Sauce*
1 pound large shrimp	1 pound linguine
1½ pounds Florida lobster tail, shelled	

Place a large pot of water on to boil. Heat oil in a saucepan. Add the vegetables and garlic and sauté over medium heat about 5 minutes. Remove the vegetables from the pan and reserve. Shell and devein the shrimp by making a slit along the back or outside of the shrimp, lifting out the black vein, and discarding it. Rinse. Cut the lobster into pieces about the same size as the shrimp. Sauté the shrimp and lobster in the saucepan for 1 minute to release their juices. Return the vegetables to the pan and add the tomato sauce, thyme, and pepper. Let simmer gently for 10 minutes. Just before serving, stir in sour cream and Dat'l Do-it Sauce. Meanwhile, add the linguine to the boiling water. Boil 9 minutes for dried or 3 minutes for fresh. Drain and toss with the sauce in a large serving bowl.

8 servings.

*Dat'l Do-it Sauce is a combination of Datil peppers from St. Augustine, Florida, tomatoes, and other spices. Datil peppers are small with a thick pulp and are very hot. To those who know peppers, they have a unique taste, adding zest and depth to the sauce. A dash of hot pepper sauce and a spoonful of Worcestershire sauce can be substituted.

CRAB

These crustaceans play an important role in Keys cuisine. Two varieties are particularly prominent—the blue crab and the stone crab.

Blue crabs can be found in salt and fresh water from Cape Cod to Florida. They are abundant in the bays and estuaries of the Gulf of Mexico and Chesapeake Bay. The solid pieces of lump meat taken from the body are justly popular in shellfish cocktails and salads. The claw meat, although a little hard to get at, is wonderful when freshly steamed and served as an hors d'oeuvre.

Stone crabs, with their large red and black claws, are a Florida institution. Only the claws are taken from the crabs when they are caught. The bodies are thrown back into the water where they will grow a new claw within about 18 months. The claws are cooked as soon as they are brought in from the fishing boats. Fresh stone crab claws cooked to order are best, but this luxury is available only to those who catch them or know someone who does. The claws cannot be reheated and take on an ammonia taste if they are. Refrigerated uncooked claws will hold 10 hours. Bring them to room temperature before cooking so that the meat won't stick to the shell. You can tell if you've been served a frozen crab claw because of its spongy texture.

To cook: Place in boiling salted water for 2½ minutes; do not overcook.

Steamed Blue Crabs

Blue crab fishing is popular in the Upper Keys, and many crabs are caught right along Card Sound Road in Key Largo. One of the best and simplest preparations is to steam them. These crabs are usually served with a cocktail or tartar sauce, but they are so sweet that I prefer them without sauce.

If you catch the crabs yourself, bring some seaweed home with you to cover the crabs while they steam. It lends extra flavor to their meat.

2 dozen blue crabs	*seaweed to cover crabs (optional)*
2 quarts water	*6 small bowls of hot cocktail or tartar sauce*
½ cup Crab Boil or Old Bay Seasoning*	*(pages 7, 13, 29, 89)*
2 lemons, quartered	

Select the crabs carefully, throwing out any that are not alive. Bring the water to a boil and add seasoning and lemon. Place a steaming basket over the water and add the crabs. Let steam 20 minutes or until the crabs are a bright orange color.

To serve, cover the table with newspapers and have plenty of napkins or paper towels on hand. Set a bowl of cocktail sauce at each place. Bring a platterful of crabs to the table and let everyone dig in. Ice cold beer goes perfectly with this meal.

6 servings.

---

*These are ready-prepared seafood seasonings made from a combination of spices such as celery salt, mustard seeds, pepper, bay leaves, cloves, allspice, ginger, mace, cardamom, cassia, and paprika. Any seafood seasoning will do.

Tugboat Crab Cakes with Tartar Sauce

Annie Jackson opened Tugboat Annie's in 1978, behind the dive shop on Seagate and Ocean Bay Drive in Key Largo. Fishermen, divers, and local residents enjoyed the good, honest local food. Annie died in 1986, and Debbie and Rick Alvarez are carrying on in her tradition. It's the type of place I love to find, off the main road, near the water, with just plain, good home-cooked food. You can eat on the screened porch and watch the fishing boats across the way at the Key Largo Fisheries.

Use either fresh or frozen crabmeat for these patties. Sea legs also work well here. Rick says the secret to these crab cakes is sautéing them in garlic butter.

1 pound crabmeat	*2 tablespoons lime juice*
¾ cup seasoned bread crumbs*	*½ teaspoon Worcestershire sauce*
3 eggs	*salt and freshly ground black pepper to taste*
¼ cup milk	*3 tablespoons butter*
¼ cup chopped fresh parsley	*2 cloves garlic, crushed*
2 tablespoons chopped scallions	*lime wedges*

Flake crabmeat. Add the remaining ingredients except the butter, garlic, and lime wedges and mix well. Chill for 30 minutes. Heat the butter in large skillet and add garlic. Shape crab mixture into eight 2½-inch patties. Sauté until browned, about 4 minutes on each side. Drain on paper towels and serve with lime wedges and tartar sauce. Rick and Debbie suggest accompanying the crab cakes with french fries and coleslaw.

8 servings.

Crab Sandwiches

Place each crab cake on a toasted hamburger bun with lettuce and tomato. Season with lime juice or tartar sauce.

---

*Season with salt, pepper, 1 teaspoon oregano, 1 clove garlic, crushed, and 1 tablespoon grated Parmesan cheese; or use a bought seasoned bread crumb mixture.

◆

Eggs Neptune

Add some chopped shrimp and lobster to the crab mixture and prepare as indicated. Place a patty on each half of a split toasted English muffin and top each patty with a poached egg and Hollandaise Sauce. Garnish with strawberries and serve for Sunday morning brunch.

◆

Tugboat's Tartar Sauce

2 cups mayonnaise
1 cup sweet pickle relish

¼ large onion, chopped
salt and pepper to taste

Mix ingredients in a bowl and taste for seasoning.
3 cups sauce.

Ziggie's Stone Crabs with Mustard Sauce

Ziggie's gets their stone crabs as soon as they are caught and serves them with this mustard sauce.

*6 pounds cooked large stone crab claws (about
   3 to 4 per person)*
2 teaspoons white vinegar
2 teaspoons dry English mustard

1 teaspoon lemon juice
1½ cups mayonnaise
few drops water
dash Tabasco sauce

Ask your fish man to crack the claws for you, or crack them at home. This makes it easier to remove the meat when they are served.

Mix the vinegar and dry mustard in a medium bowl. Add the lemon juice and then the mayonnaise. Whisk in enough water to make the sauce smooth and creamy. Taste and add Tabasco to desired degree of heat. Serve with the stone crabs.
4 servings.

KEY WEST PINK SHRIMP

If you are fortunate enough to come to the Keys, you'll have a chance to taste "pink gold," as the natives call them. These are big, juicy Key West pink shrimp. When I asked at a fish counter in Key West why the uncooked shrimp were pink, the surprised salesgirl said, "I've never seen them any other color." Fresh shrimp play a large role in Keys cuisine. Shrimping became an important industry in the Keys in the 1970's. If you don't have access to pink shrimp, these recipes will work very well with any type of fresh shrimp.

Craig's Shrimp Scampi

Craig started out in the Keys at the Pilot House. He helped to develop Harvey's Fish Sandwich, now well known and copied in the Upper Keys. Craig's Restaurant is at mile marker 90.5 and is known for its simple, freshly cooked dishes. This recipe's secret is sweet fresh shrimp.

2 pounds medium shrimp
4 tablespoons margarine (½ stick)
6 tablespoons unsalted butter (¾ stick)
salt and pepper to taste
3 cups sliced mushrooms

1½ cups sliced scallions (cut into ½-inch pieces)
3 tablespoons crushed garlic (about 6 large cloves)

Shell the shrimp and devein them by making a slit along the back or outside of the shrimp, lifting out the black vein, and discarding it. Rinse the shrimp. Melt the margarine in a large skillet. Add the shrimp and sauté for 1 minute. Add butter and salt and pepper to taste. When the butter is melted, add the mushrooms, scallions, and garlic. Cook another 2 to 3 minutes. Serve over white or yellow rice.

6 servings.

Spicy Shrimp with Mango, Avocado, and Chardonnay—Louie's Backyard

Sitting on the three-tiered deck looking out at the blue-green water, I could have been on the Italian Riviera, but the two sea hibiscus or mahoe trees forming a canopy over the deck and the hedges of silver buttonwood could be at no other place than Louie's Backyard in Key West. A gentle breeze wafted over us as we enjoyed our 2½-hour lunch. This is the genteel side of Key West.

Doug Shook and his very capable staff create recipes based on the products that are available in the area. This dish has several components. The mango-chardonnay puree can be made in the morning for the afternoon. Bring it to room temperature before serving. The avocado butter can be made 2 hours ahead. Cover tightly to keep it from turning color.

◆

Shrimp Marinade

48 large shrimp	4 cinnamon sticks
2 cups orange juice	2 tablespoons sesame oil
¼ cup lemon juice	1 tablespoon cayenne pepper
2 oranges, grated rind	½ tablespoon salt

Shell the shrimp and devein them by making a slit along the back or outside the shrimp, lifting out the black vein, and discarding it. Rinse. Combine the fruit juices, grated rind, cinnamon sticks, sesame oil, and seasonings in a stainless steel or enamel saucepan and bring to a boil. Cool. Strain into a bowl. Add the shrimp. Let marinate at least 1 hour.

◆

Mango-Chardonnay Puree

2 ripe mangos, peeled and pitted
½ cup chardonnay

¼ cup champagne vinegar
salt and freshly ground black pepper to taste

Puree the ingredients in the container of a blender or food processor until smooth. Taste and balance the acidity with more chardonnay or vinegar. If the mangos are very fibrous, strain the mixture. Hold at room temperature until the dish is assembled.

◆

Avocado Butter

2 ripe avocados, peeled and pitted
½ small red onion, diced
½ red pepper, diced
2 tablespoons chopped cilantro

1 lime, juiced
1 cup unsalted butter (2 sticks), softened
1 teaspoon salt
pinch of cayenne

Combine the ingredients in a large bowl and beat with a wooden spoon until nearly smooth, or use an electric mixer equipped with a paddle. If not using immediately, scrape into a bowl and cover the surface directly with plastic wrap. Refrigerate for no more than 2 hours.

Makes enough sauce for 1 pound pasta.

◆

Cooking and Serving

2 tablespoons olive oil   *1 pound fettuccine*
1 tablespoon butter

Place a large pot of water on to boil. Meanwhile, drain the shrimp, reserving the marinade, and heat a sauté pan until nearly smoking. Add the olive oil and butter and when hot place the shrimp in one layer in the pan. When they start to take color, turn and color the other side. Add 2 tablespoons of the marinade and toss to coat shrimp. Continue cooking the shrimp briefly until just done. Do not overcook.

Add the pasta to the boiling water and boil 1 to 2 minutes for fresh pasta or 9 minutes if using dried. The pasta should be cooked through, but firm. Drain the pasta and toss in the avocado butter. Arrange the pasta on 4 individual plates and make a well in the middle of each. Spoon ¼ cup mango puree into each well and arrange the shrimp on top. Serve immediately.

4 servings.

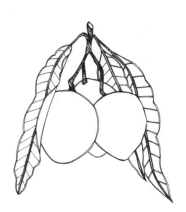

Key West Shrimp Boil with Key Lime Mustard Sauce

Key West shrimp are a treat if you can find them, but any fresh large shrimp can be used for this recipe. Dip the cooked shrimp into the Key Lime Mustard sauce. In Key West they leave the shrimp in their shells, spread newspapers on the table, and let everyone dig in.

2½ pounds large shrimp
1 12-ounce can or bottle beer

1 tablespoon Old Bay Seasoning or any fish or
   crab boil

Rinse the shrimp and drain. Pour the beer into a stainless steel pan and add the seasoning. Bring the beer to a boil and add the shrimp. As soon as the beer comes back to a boil, remove the shrimp; do not overcook. Serve immediately with the Key Lime Mustard Sauce.

6 servings.

◆

Key Lime Mustard Sauce

8 tablespoons mayonnaise
8 teaspoons American-style prepared mustard
3 tablespoons Key lime juice (lime juice may

   be substituted)
salt and freshly ground black pepper to taste

Combine the ingredients, except the salt and pepper, in a small bowl and taste. Add salt and pepper if needed. Serve with the shrimp.

Makes about ⅔ cup sauce.

Seafood Collin

Craig Belcher from Craig's Restaurant at mile marker 90.5 named this dish after an English friend's son. He says this is the only reason for its English name. Sweet scallops are combined with shrimp and served in a cream sauce. This dish can be served over rice or in a ramekin as a first course.

18 medium shrimp
18 sea scallops
½ cup butter (1 stick)
3 tomatoes, diced
3 cups sliced mushrooms

3 tablespoons crushed garlic
salt and freshly ground white pepper to taste
1 tablespoon paprika
2 cups heavy cream

Shell and devein the shrimp. Make a slit along the back or outside of the shrimp. Lift out the black vein and discard. Rinse the shrimp and scallops. Melt the butter in a large skillet. Add the tomatoes, mushrooms, and garlic and sauté 1 minute. Add the shrimp and scallops and continue to cook for another minute. Add salt and pepper to taste. Add the paprika and then the cream. Cook gently until the cream thickens, about 3 minutes. Serve over rice or in a ramekin.

6 servings.

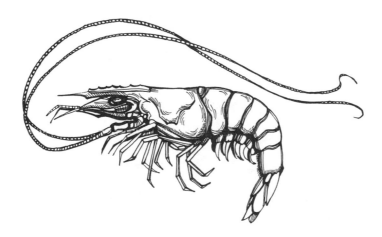

Norman Van Aken's Grilled Shrimp and Hot Sausage with Roast Garlic and Parmesan Butter

Norman Van Aken likes to bring different flavors together to form a delicate blend that plays on the palate, yet each part of the recipe can stand on its own. The marinated shrimp can be grilled and served separately. Chorizo is a type of spicy Cuban sausage made from pork and liver, but any spicy sausage can be substituted. Roast garlic goes well with grilled meats, and parmesan butter is a versatile sauce.

Note: The marinade requires overnight preparation.

◆

Shrimp Marinade

24 large shrimp
¼ cup chopped fresh parsley
¼ cup chopped fresh cilantro
¼ cup olive oil
¼ cup sherry wine vinegar
4 cloves garlic, crushed
1 tablespoon lemon juice

1 teaspoon Hungarian paprika, hot
1 teaspoon salt
½ teaspoon oregano
¼ teaspoon mace (optional)
freshly ground black pepper to taste
1 large pinch saffron (optional)

Shell the shrimp and devein them by making a slit along the back or outside of the shrimp, lifting out the black vein, and discarding it. Rinse. Combine the remaining ingredients in a medium bowl and add the shrimp. Cover and refrigerate overnight or for at least 12 hours.

◆

Roast Garlic

3 heads garlic
olive oil to cover garlic

3 bay leaves
12 black peppercorns

Preheat oven to 300 degrees. Cut off a small portion from the top of the garlic head, leaving the bulb intact. Place the garlic in a small pan and cover with olive oil. Add the bay leaves and peppercorns. Cover with foil and bake 45 minutes. The garlic should be soft. Remove from the oven and allow to cool. Squeeze the cloves from their skins. Reserve the oil for another use.

◆

Parmesan Butter Sauce

1½ tablespoons olive oil
3 shallots, finely chopped
½ cup white wine vinegar
5 sprigs fresh thyme
1 bay leaf, broken in half

½ cup heavy cream
2 cups ice-cold unsalted butter (4 sticks)
2 to 3 tablespoons Parmesan, freshly grated
freshly ground black pepper to taste

Heat the olive oil in a small saucepan and sauté the shallots for several minutes. Add the vinegar, thyme, and bay leaf and reduce until a glaze. Add the cream and reduce by one-third. Cut the cold butter into pieces and whisk into the reduced cream piece by piece to make a thick creamy sauce. Strain and add the cheese. Season with pepper to taste and serve immediately.

About 4½ cups sauce.

◆

Cooking and Serving

½ pound chorizo or any other type of sausage   *½ cup grated Parmesan*

Remove the shrimp from the marinade. Cut the sausage into 1-inch rounds. Preheat grill or broiler. Grill or broil shrimp and sausage 3 to 4 minutes. Ladle some sauce onto individual plates. Divide the shrimp and sausage into four portions and place on sauce. Surround with Roast Garlic and pass grated Parmesan around with the plates.

4 servings.

Key West Shrimp on Toasted Cumin Butter with Black Beans and Chili, Pineapple, and Coconut Relish

Norman Van Aken calls this "fusion" cooking. This type of cuisine combines historic, ethnic foods with classic techniques and modern ideas. In this recipe fresh Keys shrimp are served with Cuban black beans and garnished with a tropical fruit relish, as pleasing to the eye as to the palate.

The black beans can be made up to three days ahead and can be reheated and served when needed. The recipe calls for Spanish olive oil, which has a slightly peppery taste when compared with other olive oils. The recipe works well with any good-quality extra virgin olive oil. The black bean and relish recipes call for poblano peppers. These may be difficult to find, any semihot pepper will do. Mace is the outer covering of the nutmeg. Its flavor is between that of nutmeg and cinnamon.

Note: The marinade requires overnight preparation.

◆

Shrimp Marinade

30 large shrimp	2 tablespoons Spanish olive oil
2 tablespoons chopped parsley	½ teaspoon hot Hungarian paprika
2 tablespoons chopped cilantro	½ teaspoon sea salt
2 cloves garlic, crushed	¼ teaspoon ground mace
½ lemon, juiced	1 teaspoon freshly ground black peppercorns
2 tablespoons semidry sherry	1 pinch of saffron

Shell the shrimp and devein them by making a slit along the back or outside of the shrimp, lifting out the black vein, and discarding it. Rinse. Mix the remaining ingredients in a large bowl. Add the shrimp, cover, and refrigerate overnight.

◆

Black Beans

1 cup dried black beans
2 ounces smoked slab bacon, rind removed, diced
1 tablespoon olive oil
2 jalapeño peppers, seeded and diced
1 poblano pepper, diced
½ yellow pepper, diced
½ green pepper, diced
½ small red onion, diced
1 stalk celery, diced

2 cloves garlic, crushed
1 small smoked pork hock or ¾ pound pork hock or smoked boneless ham
1 tablespoon fresh thyme or ½ tablespoon dried
1 tablespoon ground cumin
1 bay leaf
¼ cup Madeira wine
2½ cups chicken stock
1 teaspoon freshly ground black peppercorns
salt to taste

Soak the beans in water overnight. Add the bacon and olive oil to a large heavy-bottomed saucepan. Sauté until the bacon is translucent. Add the vegetables and garlic. Reduce heat and simmer, stirring, for several minutes. Add the pork hock, thyme, cumin, and bay leaf and continue to stir several minutes. Drain the beans and add to the saucepan, cooking 2 to 3 more minutes. Add the Madeira and cook another minute. Add the stock and black pepper, making sure the stock covers the beans by at least 1 inch. Simmer until the beans are tender, approximately 2½ to 3 hours. Season to taste. Remove the pork hock from the beans. Cut off the meat and return it to the beans. To intensify the flavor of the beans, strain off their liquid into another saucepan and reduce liquid over high heat to concentrate the flavors; pour the reduced liquid over the beans. This also gives a deeper, more dramatic color.

◆

Chili, Pineapple, and Coconut Relish

1 poblano chili pepper, diced
½ yellow pepper, diced
½ cup fresh coconut, diced

¼ red onion, diced
2 tablespoons sherry vinegar
sprigs fresh cilantro

Combine the ingredients except cilantro in a small bowl and let stand at room temperature while the flavors blend. Set aside sprigs of cilantro for garnish. This can be made up to 8 hours in advance.

◆

Toasted Cumin Butter

1 tablespoon cumin seeds, freshly toasted
1 clove garlic, crushed
6 tablespoons white wine
3 tablespoons white wine vinegar
2 shallots, peeled and sliced
1 bay leaf

1 teaspoon cracked black pepper
½ cup heavy cream
1 cup ice-cold unsalted butter (2 sticks)
½ teaspoon lime juice
salt and pepper to taste

Place the cumin seeds and garlic in a mortar and pestle and pound together. Combine the garlic mixture, white wine, vinegar, shallots, bay leaf, and pepper in a small saucepan and reduce the liquid to a few tablespoons. Add the cream and reduce by one-third. Just before serving, cut the butter into small pieces and whisk in piece by piece, until it is all incorporated. Wait for each piece to be incorporated before adding the next. Strain the sauce and add lime juice, salt, and pepper. Taste for seasoning and add more lime juice if necessary.

◆

Cooking and Serving

Oil the grill grate and preheat. Drain the shrimp and grill about 5 minutes. Spoon about 2 tablespoons of the black beans onto the center of each plate. Spoon the cumin butter around the beans. Divide the shrimp into 6 portions and arrange with the thick end on the beans and the tail end in the butter. Sprinkle with the Chili, Pineapple, and Coconut Relish and garnish with fresh cilantro sprigs.

6 servings.

GRUNT

Just drop a line in any shallow water near a coral reef and you'll come up with a grunt, so called because they make a grunting sound when caught. They're small, and you need about three to make one light portion, but their sweet white meat is delicious.

Grits and Grunts

Bob and Clara Hardin, while living on their boat, the *Mystic Turtle,* in the Keys, used to catch grunts for breakfast. Even four-year-old Casey had to drop a line for his breakfast. Here is Bob's recipe.

2 pounds grunt, grouper, or other white fish fillets	*4 cups water*
½ cup milk	*1 teaspoon salt*
1 egg	*1 cup quick grits*
salt and freshly ground black pepper to taste	*¼ cup grated cheddar or Emmentaler*
2 cups flour or seasoned bread crumbs	*salt and pepper to taste*
vegetable oil for frying	*lime wedges or Old Sour (see Glossary)*

Carefully fillet the grunts if you've caught your own. Or ask your fish man for fillets. Mix the milk and egg in a medium bowl. Soak the fillets in the liquid and drain. Lightly salt the fillets and mix salt and pepper into the flour. Dip the fillets in the flour and shake off any excess. Pour the oil into a pan for deep-frying and heat to 350 degrees. Fry about 3 fillets at a time for 3 to 4 minutes. Drain on paper towels or, as Clara did on her boat, on brown paper bags. Continue to fry the fish until all are ready. Meanwhile, bring the water and 1 teaspoon salt to a boil and gradually add the grits, stirring constantly for 3 to 5 minutes or until the water is absorbed. Remove from the heat and stir in the cheese. Add salt and pepper to taste. Serve the grits and grunts hot with some fresh lime wedges or Old Sour to sprinkle on top.

6 servings.

SHARK

Shark must be handled properly from the minute it is caught. The head and tail should be removed and the fish cleaned immediately, with salt water flushed through its veins. Otherwise, it will develop an ammonia taste that is usually disguised by soaking in lemon juice or milk. If the shark smells sweet when you buy it, then it's fine. Mako is the best type to buy; lemon and black tip shark are also good.

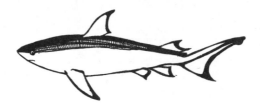

Tugboat's Fried Shark Basket

Tugboat's is right across the street from the fishing docks and Rick Alvarez knows how to buy his shark. It's always good there. Fried shark strips are tender, juicy, and easy to make.

2 pounds shark　　　　　　　*2 cloves garlic, crushed*
3 eggs　　　　　　　　　　*2 teaspoons salt*
1 cup water　　　　　　　*½ teaspoon freshly ground black pepper*
½ cup cornmeal　　　　　*oil for frying*
½ cup flour

Cut the shark into about 30 strips, 5 per person. Mix the eggs and water in a bowl. Combine the cornmeal, flour, garlic, salt, and pepper in a second bowl. Dip the strips into the egg wash and then into the flour mixture to lightly coat. Heat oil to 350 degrees and fry about 5 strips at a time for about 4 minutes or until golden. Drain on paper towels. These are good served with curly french fries and coleslaw.

6 servings.

Marker 88's Everglades Frogs' Legs with Garlic Butter

André Mueller gets his frogs' legs directly from the men who catch them in the Everglades. They are abundant there and André knows they're fresh. When buying yours, be sure to choose legs that are approximately the same size so they will cook evenly and for the same length of time. This avoids overcooking the smaller pieces and undercooking the larger ones.

28 frogs' legs (6 to 8 per person)
1 teaspoon salt
1 teaspoon white pepper
2 tablespoons lime juice
1 tablespoon Worcestershire sauce
2 eggs

2 tablespoons milk
2 tablespoons oil
flour
2 tablespoons clarified butter (see Glossary) or
    1 tablespoon butter and 1 tablespoon oil
Garlic Butter (recipe follows)

Rinse and season legs with salt and pepper. Mix lime juice and Worcestershire in a bowl. In a second bowl, mix eggs, milk, and oil. Dip the frogs' legs in lime juice and then in flour, shaking the excess off; there should be only a very thin coat of flour. Dip the legs in egg wash. Heat the butter in a skillet and sauté the legs for 2 minutes. Turn and sauté another 2 minutes. Don't overcook or the meat will separate from the bones. Serve with garlic butter either spooned over legs or on the side for dipping.

4 servings.

Garlic Butter

½ cup butter (1 stick)
1 tablespoon crushed garlic
¼ teaspoon chopped shallots
2 teaspoons chopped fresh parsley

1 tablespoon white wine
1 teaspoon lemon juice
¼ teaspoon white pepper

Heat the butter very slowly in a saucepan; it should still be thick. Briskly whip in garlic, shallots, and parsley. Place in the refrigerator until ready to use; it should be cold for the next step. Remove from refrigerator and whip in the white wine and lemon juice over very low heat. If the heat is too high, the butter will break down and separate. Add pepper to taste. Serve immediately.

Makes about ½ cup sauce.

André's Gator Steak

Alligator is native to this area of the world. In the past, it was used for its hide and sometimes its meat. While today game is back in style, alligator meat is usually farmed. Ask for farmed alligator tail at your nearest specialty food store and have a gator party.

1½ pounds alligator tail
2 tablespoons lime juice
1 tablespoon Worcestershire sauce
2 eggs
2 tablespoons milk

2 tablespoons oil
2 tablespoons clarified butter (see Glossary) or
*   1 tablespoon butter and 1 tablespoon oil*
Garlic Butter (see previous recipe)

Cut alligator into 4 medallions (steaks). Mix the lime juice and Worcestershire sauce in a bowl. In a second bowl, mix the eggs, milk, and oil. Dip the steaks in lime juice and then in flour. Shake excess flour off; there should be a very thin coat of flour on steak. Dip in egg wash. Heat butter in skillet and sauté steaks for 2 minutes. Turn and sauté another 2 minutes. Don't overcook. Serve with garlic butter either spooned over the gator steak or on the side for dipping. Or, use your favorite seafood dipping sauce.

4 servings.

GROUPER

Groupers are members of the sea bass family and are commonly found around the coral reefs and rock outcroppings of the inner coastal shelf. Groupers are white-fleshed and lean and fillet very well. Because the skin is tough and strong flavored, the fillets are usually cooked skinned. The flesh is firm, fries and poaches well, and retains its shape and moisture when cut into fingers and deep-fried. Groupers make a wonderful fish chowder that is especially good when the heads are used for making the stock.

Tom McGuane's Sour-Orange Grouper

The writer and director Tom McGuane has lived in Key West off and on for the last twenty years. His novel about Key West, *Ninety-Two in the Shade,* was made into a movie that he wrote and directed. This is his recipe.

The sour oranges called for here are difficult to find, although they are available in Hispanic markets and specialty food shops in January and February. Substitute half orange, half lime juice for the sour-orange juice. Any type of firm fish, such as halibut or monkfish, can be used in this recipe.

4 grouper fillets, skinned (about 1½ pounds)	*⅓ cup scallions, chopped*
1 cup sour-orange juice	*1 tablespoon crushed garlic*
⅓ cup milk	*½ cup unsalted butter (1 stick)*
¼ cup flour	*4 lemon slices*
¼ cup peanut oil	*4 sour-orange slices*
¼ cup olive oil	*basil or parsley sprigs*

Marinate the fillets in ½ cup of the sour-orange juice for 1 hour. Remove and dry with paper towels. Marinate in the milk for 15 minutes. Dredge in the flour and shake off any excess. Pour the peanut and olive oils into a large skillet and fry the scallions and garlic. When the garlic starts to turn a golden brown, remove the garlic and scallions with a slotted spoon and reserve. Add the fish to the pan and fry the fillets until they are golden on each side (allow about 10 minutes to cook a fillet that is about 1 inch thick). Remove the fish to a warm serving platter and cover with foil to keep warm.

Melt the butter in the skillet, stirring constantly. Add the reserved scallions and garlic along with the remaining ½ cup sour-orange juice. Let the juice warm in the pan for a minute, and then spoon the sauce over the fish fillets. Garnish with a slice of lemon and a slice of orange for each fillet and decorate with the basil or parsley sprigs on the outer rim of the platter.

4 servings.

Manny and Isa's Fried Grouper Fingers

The grouper's firm white flesh makes it a perfect choice for cutting into pieces and frying. Use any firm fish, such as cod, as a substitute. Baked potatoes, rice and black beans, or french fries are served with the fish at Manny and Isa's Restaurant in Islamorada.

1½ pounds skinned grouper fillets
2 tablespoons lime juice
4 cloves garlic, crushed
1 teaspoon salt
1 teaspoon white pepper
½ cup milk
1 egg

½ cup all-purpose flour
1 cup fine cracker meal
3 to 4 cups oil for frying (depending on the size of pot)
4 to 5 washed lettuce leaves
4 tablespoons chopped fresh parsley

Cut the grouper into 1-ounce fingers about 1 × 3 inches and sprinkle with lime juice. Rub them with a little garlic and salt and pepper. Whisk the egg and milk in a bowl. Dip the fingers into liquid and then roll in flour. Dip in liquid again and then roll in cracker meal. Heat oil to 350 degrees. Fry fish for 5 to 8 minutes, adding one finger at a time, and adding subsequent pieces as the oil comes back to temperature. Serve on a bed of lettuce, sprinkled with chopped parsley.

4 servings.

Manny and Isa's Spanish Fish with Cuban Sauce

Grouper, yellowtail, and dolphin are delivered daily to Manny and Isa's restaurant. The fish is so fresh that they need only be quickly broiled and served with this Cuban sauce.

◆

Cuban Sauce

2 large cans tomato sauce (15 ounces each)   2 cloves garlic, crushed
2 cups diced onions   2 teaspoons ground cumin
2 green peppers, diced   ½ teaspoon oregano
2 whole red pimentos, diced   ½ teaspoon freshly ground black pepper

Combine the sauce ingredients in a large saucepan, cover, and simmer gently for 20 minutes. Taste for seasoning and add more pepper, oregano, or cumin if necessary.

◆

Fish Preparation

6 8-ounce grouper or yellowtail fillets or 2½   2 tablespoons oil
   pounds dolphin fillets

Preheat broiler for about 10 minutes. Brush a little oil over the fillets. Place on a baking tray and broil 10 to 15 minutes. Figure about 8 minutes per inch of thickness, measured at the thickest part of the fillet. Do not turn the fish; it will cook through on the hot broiler. In Manny and Isa's restaurant they serve the fish on a bed of white rice with the sauce spooned over the top and a salad and good Cuban bread on the side.

4 servings.

YELLOWTAIL SNAPPER

This shallow-water snapper is easily recognized by the yellow stripe running the length of its body. Its white delicate flesh does not keep well, even when placed on ice; the fresher the better. Yellowtails are so sweet that just pan frying them in a little butter and a splash of lime juice produces a treat.

Lorelei Yellowtail with Lime Pepper Sauce

At one time, the tracks of Flagler's railroad ran right past the Lorelei Restaurant. Cargoes from boats were transferred to freight cars for shipment north and south. Today, some railroad ties and track are still visible in the water off the docking area. Many of the backcountry fishing guides use the Lorelei as their base, and it is a great spot to catch-up on all of the local fishing tales. John Maloughney has just remodeled the restaurant and kitchen there. He created this recipe, which is tart and spicy and very simple to make. Use a light, flaky fish such as sole or flounder if you can't find yellowtail.

◆

Lime Pepper Sauce

1 cup heavy cream	1 teaspoon clam juice
½ cup fresh lime juice	dash Tabasco
1 tablespoon cracked black pepper	2 tablespoons butter
1 teaspoon sugar	1½ teaspoons flour

Heat the cream and add the lime juice; warm just to a simmer, but do not boil. Add the black pepper, sugar, clam juice, and Tabasco. Mash the butter and flour together and stir by small pieces into the sauce to thicken. Blend in well. The sauce should be smooth and just cling to the spoon. Set aside.

Makes about 1½ cups sauce.

◆

Yellowtail

1½ pounds yellowtail fillets	1 tablespoon butter
salt and freshly ground black pepper	4 sprigs fresh parsley
¼ cup flour	1 lime, sliced

Sprinkle the fillets with salt and pepper and dredge in flour, shaking off any excess. Melt the butter in a skillet and add the fish fillets. Sauté until golden brown, turning once during the cooking. This should take about 8 minutes. Place the fish on individual plates and spoon the sauce on top. Garnish with a sprig of parsley and a slice of lime.

4 servings.

Yellowtail with Key Lime Butter—The Pier House

Michael Kulow at The Pier House in Key West serves this delicate fish with his light Keys version of a traditional beurre blanc. The tart Key lime gives the sauce its punch, but regular limes can be used. If yellowtail isn't available, substitute any light white fish fillets. Yellowtail fillets will vary in size. Figure about 6 to 8 ounces of fish per person. The delicate flavor of the yellowtail should not be smothered by the sauce; serve just a small amount with the fish.

◆

Key Lime Butter

½ cup white wine
1 tablespoon shallots, chopped
¼ cup Key lime juice

1 cup heavy cream
½ cup cold unsalted butter (1 stick)

Place wine, shallots, and Key lime juice in a saucepan and reduce over high heat by one-third. Add the cream and reduce again by one-third. Remove from heat and add the butter one piece at a time, stirring constantly. As each piece melts, add another piece. This way the temperature of the sauce will remain constant and the butter will bind and thicken it. Place its pan in a pan of hot water to keep warm while cooking the fish.

◆

Yellowtail

2¼ to 2½ pounds yellowtail fillets
¼ cup flour seasoned with salt and white
* pepper*

2 tablespoons unsalted butter
1 ripe avocado, thinly sliced
1 ripe papaya, thinly sliced

Dip the fillets in the seasoned flour, shaking off the excess. Melt the butter in a large skillet and add the fish, moving each piece as it touches the pan. This will prevent it from sticking. Brown for 1 minute. Turn and brown the second side. Reduce the heat and sauté 4 to 5 minutes. Do not overcook or it will become dry.

Place the fillets on individual plates and spoon a little sauce over them. Garnish each plate with thin slices of avocado and papaya.

6 servings.

Yellowtail "Marie Ellen"

George Hommel is a Keys personality. As President Bush's personal fishing guide, he helps to make the arrangements for the President's fishing breaks. When George asked André Mueller from Marker 88 to cook a dinner for the President, André named the main course after George Hommel's daughter, Marie Ellen. The dinner was served on the President's April 21, 1990, fishing trip to Islamorada.

André suggests that you place all of the fish in one large pot with the white wine and water. The shell fish will open in just a few minutes and provide a strong base for the sauce. When cooking fish together this way, be careful not to overcook the more delicate fish. If you are unable to find all of the fish, substitute whatever is fresh and available to you. Maine lobster or crab can be used instead of Florida lobster, and large shrimp instead of Key West pinks.

2½ pounds yellowtail fillets
2 Florida lobster tails, scrubbed
1 pound bay scallops
12 littleneck clams, scrubbed
12 Key West pink shrimp
12 mussels, scrubbed
2 cups water

1 cup white wine
2 tablespoons butter
1½ tablespoons flour
1 cup light cream
a few strands of saffron dissolved in 2
*   tablespoons hot water*
salt and freshly ground white pepper to taste

Shell and devein the shrimp. Make a slit along the back or outside of the shrimp. Lift out the black vein and discard. Rinse. Place the seafood in a large pot with the water and white wine. Cover and bring to a simmer; cook for 3 to 4 minutes, then remove the shrimp and scallops. Check the yellowtail and remove when no longer translucent, after 6 to 7 minutes. Remove the clams and mussels when they open, about 7 minutes. The lobster should be cooked for about 15 minutes or until it turns red and the flesh is opaque. Remove the shell and cut the lobster into small pieces. Place the fillets on a warm serving platter and arrange the rest of the seafood around the fillets. Cover with a piece of foil to keep warm.

Melt the butter in a saucepan and add the flour to make a loose paste. If the paste is thick, add a little more butter. Strain the fish liquid into the saucepan, stirring to make a smooth sauce. Add the cream. Add the saffron in hot water to the sauce. Season with salt and pepper to taste. Spoon some of the sauce over the fish and serve the rest in a sauceboat.

6 servings.

Seafood Lasagna

When Kathy Hughson arrived in Marathon, she was overwhelmed by the abundance of fresh seafood and decided to revamp some of her favorite dishes. Her love of cheese, pasta, and seafood inspired the creation of this dish. The smoked gouda in the sauce gives the impression of smoked fish.

◆

Cream Sauce

6 tablespoons butter (¾ stick)
1 small onion, chopped
1 tablespoon chopped garlic
6 tablespoons flour
2 6.5-ounce cans chopped clams (including juice)
1 pint half-and-half
1 cup whole milk

1 cup grated smoked gouda (4 ounces)
½ cup grated cheddar cheese (2 ounces)
¼ cup grated Parmesan (1 ounce)
¾ teaspoon thyme
½ teaspoon oregano
½ teaspoon salt
¼ teaspoon white pepper

Melt the butter in a large saucepan. Add the onions and sauté until golden; add the garlic. Whisk in flour to make a thick smooth paste. Cook 1 minute without browning. Remove from

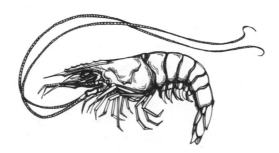

heat. Whisk in clams with juice, half-and-half, and milk. Return to heat and simmer gently until the sauce thickens, stirring constantly. Add the cheeses all at once and continue stirring until melted. Add seasonings and simmer for 3 minutes, stirring. The sauce will be the consistency of a thick chowder. Set aside.

◆

Lasagna

1 pound lasagna noodles
½ pound fresh medium shrimp
1½ pounds yellowtail fillets
2¼ cups chopped fresh spinach

2 small tomatoes, chopped
½ cup grated Parmesan
9″ × 13″ baking dish

Preheat the oven to 350 degrees. Bring a large pot of water to a boil and cook lasagna for 8 to 10 minutes. Drain and rinse in cold water. Spread out on countertop. Shell and devein the shrimp. Make a slit along the back or outside of the shrimp. Lift out the black vein and discard. Rinse. If the shrimp are large, cut in half lengthwise.

Spoon a thin layer of sauce in the bottom of baking dish. Place a layer of lasagna noodles on top. Spoon more sauce on the noodles and top with the yellowtail fillets to form a single layer. Cover the fish with a second layer of noodles. Spread 2 cups of the chopped spinach and the tomatoes over the noodles. Cover with half the remaining sauce and sprinkle with ¼ cup of the Parmesan. Top with a final layer of noodles. Arrange the shrimp in single layer over the noodles. Spoon the remaining sauce over the shrimp and sprinkle the remaining spinach and Parmesan on top. Cover with foil and bake for 35 minutes. Remove foil and bake an additional 10 minutes.

Kathy likes to let the lasagna sit for 3 to 4 hours before serving so that it will cut better; it rewarms well in the microwave. It can, however, be served right out of the oven with all of the layers blending together. It can, also, be made a day ahead and reheated.

8 to 10 servings.

Snook's Fish Special

Pat Mathias says this special is one of the most popular fish dishes at Snook's Bayside Club. Snook's started out as a small café, dedicated to using the best ingredients and serving fine food. They soon moved to a waterfront location. You can sit and watch the ducks and pelicans play while the sun sets.

This is a simple, quick, and easy recipe. The secret is fresh fish. Use any type of delicate white fish, if yellowtail isn't available. This recipe fills one ramekin. Simply alter the ingredients for as many servings as you need.

4 ounces yellowtail fillets
½ Florida lobster tail, shelled
½ teaspoon chopped shallot
½ teaspoon crushed garlic
1 tablespoon peeled and chopped tomato
1 tablespoon white wine

½ teaspoon lemon juice
1 teaspoon unsalted butter
salt and freshly ground white pepper to taste
1 teaspoon chopped scallion
1 tablespoon grated Swiss cheese

Preheat the oven to 400 degrees. Cut the yellowtail and lobster into bite-size pieces. Combine the ingredients, except the scallions and cheese, in a ramekin, cover with foil, and bake 10 minutes. Remove the foil and sprinkle with scallions and cheese. Place under a hot broiler to melt and slightly color the cheese. Slip the food out of the ramekin onto a warmed plate and serve.

1 serving.

Snapper Rangoon

Bananas, papayas, and mangoes all grow in the Keys area. André Mueller combines these tropical treats and serves them with any type of white fish—snapper, yellowtail, or dolphin—at Marker 88. The sauce is sweet, and the dish has become popular in the Upper Keys.

2 pounds snapper or other white fish	2 tablespoons milk
2 tablespoons lime juice	2 tablespoons oil
1 tablespoon Worcestershire sauce	½ cup flour
½ teaspoon salt	½ teaspoon cinnamon
½ teaspoon white pepper	2 tablespoons clarified butter (see Glossary) or
2 eggs	1 tablespoon butter and 1 tablespoon oil

Preheat oven to 450 degrees. Sprinkle the fish with lime juice, Worcestershire, salt, and pepper. Combine the eggs, milk, and oil in a bowl. In a second bowl combine flour and cinnamon. Dip the fish in flour and then in the egg mixture. Heat the clarified butter in a skillet and sauté the fish on one side only. Place fillets on baking sheet, browned side up, and bake for 8 to 10 minutes.

◆

Rangoon Sauce

4 tablespoons butter (½ stick)	papaya, and mango
½ cup each, diced banana, pineapple,	½ tablespoon red currant jelly

Melt the butter in a skillet and add the diced fruit. Turn fruit carefully with a fork to keep it from breaking up. Cream the jelly with a spoon to soften it and add to the pan. Stir gently for a few minutes.

To serve, place the fish on a warmed serving platter or individual dishes and spoon the sauce over the top.

4 servings.

Manny and Isa's Fried Snapper Fillets

With so much fresh fish available in the Keys, it is easy for Manny and Isa to have it delivered to their restaurant in Islamorada each day. If the fish is fresh, it will stay together, fry well, and taste wonderful.

1½ pounds snapper or firm white fish fillets
1 tablespoon lime juice
2 cloves garlic, crushed
1 teaspoon salt
½ cup milk
1 egg

½ cup all-purpose flour
1 cup fine cracker meal
3 to 4 cups oil for frying, depending on the
* size of pot*
4 or 5 washed lettuce leaves
4 tablespoons chopped fresh parsley

Sprinkle the fillets with lime juice and rub them with a little garlic and salt. Whisk the milk and egg together. Dip the fillets in liquid and then in flour. Dip in liquid again and roll in cracker meal. Heat oil to 350 degrees, and fry fish for 5 to 10 minutes, adding one fillet at a time. As the oil comes back to temperature, add the next fillet until all are cooked. Serve on a bed of lettuce, sprinkled with parsley. Baked potatoes, rice and black beans, or french fries are served with the fish at Manny and Isa's.

4 servings.

Dottie Hill's Baked Hog Snapper

Walk into the Key Largo Fisheries around five o'clock in the afternoon and you'll see the Bucket Brigade coming in. These are local fishermen with their catch of the day.

"They're really out there for the sport and all they're looking for is enough money to go out fishing the next day. You never know what fish will be coming in, but it's all fresh," says Dottie Hill, who has worked at the Key Largo Fisheries for more years than she wants to count. Dottie's knowledge of the fish from the Upper Keys is highly regarded. If coaxed, she will give advice on how to cook them.

An easy recipe is always appreciated at the end of a long work day. This recipe was inspired by Dottie's thoughts as she showed me around the fishery.

Hog snapper, also called hogfish, is considered the tastiest of the snapper family.

2½ pounds hog snapper or any white fish fillets	*2 green peppers, thinly sliced*
2 tablespoons oil	*2 tomatoes, thinly sliced*
½ cup fresh thyme or 1 tablespoon dried	*1 medium onion, thinly sliced*
3 cloves garlic, crushed	*4 slices Provolone cheese*

Preheat oven to 450 degrees. Place fish fillets in roasting pan. Brush with oil and sprinkle with the thyme, garlic, and vegetables. Bake 15 minutes for ¾-inch-thick fish (longer for thicker fish). Remove and place cheese slices on top. Bake a further 3 to 4 minutes. Serve immediately.

6 servings.

Frances Wolfson's Baked Red Snapper

Colonel Mitchell Wolfson, Sr., was born in Key West in 1900. Although his family moved to Miami in 1915, they retained close ties to Key West. He and his wife, Frances, launched a renaissance in the "Old Island City." They saved the old neglected house where John James Audubon painted in 1832, and today the Audubon House is lovingly maintained as a museum by their son, Mitchell Wolfson, Jr. Their restoration sparked an entire movement that saved many old homes in historic Key West. The National Trust for Historic Preservation acclaimed the Audubon House as "The outstanding restoration of its type in the United States."

When Colonel Wolfson moved to Miami from Key West he brought with him a love of Florida seafood. I found his recipe for red snapper as I was looking through Frances's old recipe box.

1 whole red snapper (about 5 pounds with head)	*1 5½-ounce jar pimentos, drained and diced*
4 tablespoons butter or margarine (½ stick), melted	*1 tablespoon lemon juice*
	1 tablespoon Worcestershire sauce
3 stalks celery, finely sliced	*2 teaspoons sugar*
½ medium onion, finely sliced	*1 teaspoon Tabasco sauce (or other chili sauce)*
1 15-ounce can tomato sauce	*salt and freshly ground black pepper to taste*
	1 lemon, sliced into wedges

Preheat oven to 350 degrees. Ask your fish man to gut and clean the fish, but leave the head and tail on. Rinse the whole fish and place in a roasting pan or baking dish, just large enough to fit the fish. Pour the butter over the fish. Combine the remaining ingredients, except the lemon wedges, and taste for seasoning. Add more Tabasco or sugar as needed. Salt and pepper to taste. Pour the sauce over the fish and bake for 45 minutes. To test for doneness, stick the point of a knife into the middle of the fish and pull some of the flesh aside; it should be opaque, not translucent. If not done, bake 5 to 10 minutes longer. It should take about 10 minutes per pound to bake. To serve, remove the fish from the pan and cut two or three servings from the top side. Place on individual plates. Remove the bone and cut the second side into sections and place on plates. Spoon the sauce over the fish and serve, garnished with lemon wedges.

4 to 6 servings.

DOLPHIN

Dolphins fished off the coast of Florida are a light white fish that should not be confused with the mammal of the same name. It is also called mahi mahi. On my first trip to the Keys, I was introduced to this delicious, flaky fish by my next-door neighbor. Everyday around five, his boat would return to his dock and he would start to clean his catch. When the pelicans began to congregate, waiting for leftover tidbits, I knew he was back. One day I finally asked him what type of fish he caught. On many evenings after that, I found a beautifully cleaned fillet of dolphin on my doorstep.

Keys Grilled Meunière à Trois

Yellowtail, dolphin, and tenderized conch make this a Keys treat. Marc Green came to the Keys from Rhode Island and combined his own special brand of New England cooking with local Keys ingredients at the Holiday Isle Restaurant. Marc uses a grill (griddle) to do most of his sautéing. His secret to a light meunière sauce is whipping the butter until it is light and fluffy before using it.

½ cup butter (1 stick) at room temperature
¾ pound yellowtail fillets
¾ pound dolphin fillets
¾ pound conch, cut into four pieces

1 tablespoon Key lime, plain lime, or lemon
juice
1 tablespoon chopped fresh parsley
salt and freshly ground white pepper to taste

Ask for conch to be put through tenderizer when you buy it. Whip the butter until it is light and fluffy and heat in a skillet or on a griddle. Add the yellowtail, dolphin, and conch and sauté over medium heat 6 to 8 minutes, turning once. Spoon Key lime juice around the edges of the fish as they cook. The sauce will be frothy. Remove from heat and sprinkle with chopped parsley and salt and pepper to taste. Serve the fish immediately with the sauce spooned over.

4 servings.

Grilled Dolphin with Tropical Fruit Salsa and Cinnamon Plantains

Norman Van Aken uses the abundance of tropical fruits in the Keys and his extensive knowledge of Cuban cuisine to create his own style, which he calls New World Cuisine. The freshness of the salsa blends well with the fish and makes a very attractive dish. If dolphin (mahi mahi) is unavailable, substitute tuna or swordfish.

The plantains (see Glossary) in this recipe are sautéed and need to be very ripe. Choose black ones at the market or let them ripen at home. If you have a yellow plantain that is not quite ripe yet, place it in a 300-degree oven until it turns black and the skin begins to split. This only works with plantains that have already started to turn yellow. Bananas can be substituted, but are softer and should be handled carefully during cooking.

◆

Dolphin Marinade

1 cup safflower or corn oil
½ cup olive oil
½ cup soy sauce
⅓ cup fresh orange juice
¼ cup fresh lemon juice

2 tablespoons fresh lime juice
1 small bunch fresh cilantro
6 black peppercorns
2 bay leaves
2 large cloves garlic, halved

Combine the ingredients and let steep for at least 1 hour to blend the flavors before using.

◆

Tropical Fruit Salsa

½ cup diced, peeled, and seeded tomatoes
½ cup diced papaya
¼ cup diced pineapple
½ cup lime or raspberry vinegar

½ cup coarsely chopped red onion
¼ cup chopped fresh cilantro
2 tablespoons olive oil

Cut the fruit into a medium-size bowl, catching their juices. Strain the resulting juices into a saucepan with the vinegar. Place over medium heat and reduce to about ⅓ cup. Add the reduced juices to the fruit with the onion, cilantro, and olive oil, and gently mix together. Taste and add more vinegar if necessary. The salsa should have a sweet and pungent flavor. The amount of vinegar needed depends on the ripeness of the fruit.

◆

Cinnamon Plantains

1 or 2 ripe plantains	*½ teaspoon freshly ground black pepper*
¼ cup flour	*2 tablespoons clarified butter (see Glossary) or*
2 teaspoons cinnamon	*1 tablespoon butter and 1 tablespoon oil*
½ teaspoon salt	

Peel the plantains and cut into diagonal slices about ¼ inch thick. Mix the flour with the cinnamon, salt, and pepper. Dredge the plantains in the flour, tapping off any excess. Heat a large sauté pan and add the clarified butter. Sauté the plantains until golden brown on each side. Remove from the pan and sprinkle with salt and pepper. Set aside.

◆

Cooking and Serving

6 7-ounce each pieces boneless, skinless dolphin

Marinate the dolphin 5 minutes. Preheat the grill and cook the fish about 5 to 8 minutes for medium-rare. The fish will be just cooked all the way through and still moist. The dolphin may also be cooked in a preheated broiler for the same amount of time. To serve, place the fish on a warm plate and top with the salsa. Add a little butter to the sauté pan and gently reheat the plantains. Surround the fish with the warm plantains.

6 servings.

Tropical Sweet-and-Sour Dolphin

My fascination with the carambola, or star fruit, drew me to create this easy recipe. When it is whole, the star fruit looks something like a short squat banana with fins. When it is cut across, the slices look like yellow stars. They have a fresh fragrance and a sweet and tart flavor, which adds zest to the sauce. Star fruit is in season from August through February and can be found in most supermarkets and specialty food stores throughout the United States. If fresh dolphin (mahi mahi) is not available, you may want to try this sauce with your favorite fresh local fish.

2½ pounds dolphin
2 tablespoons corn or safflower oil
1 tablespoon butter or margarine
1 medium onion, thinly sliced

4 ripe carambolas, rinsed
½ cup water
3 teaspoons sugar

Preheat the grill or broiler, and brush the fish with oil. If using a charcoal or gas grill, raise the grates so the fish cooks over medium heat. If broiling the fish, line a baking dish with foil and place the fish at least 5 inches from the heat. Grill or broil the dolphin for about 15 minutes, turning the fish once during cooking. The fish is done when the flesh is no longer translucent.

While the fish is cooking, heat the butter in a heavy-bottomed saucepan and gently sauté the onion slices until they are transparent, about 10 minutes. Dice two of the carambolas and slice the other two. Add the diced carambolas, water, and sugar to the onion. Let simmer until the fruit is soft, about 5 minutes. Taste for sweetness. The sweet-and-sour taste will depend on the type of carambolas you use; more sugar may be needed. Add the sliced carambolas to the sauce and let them warm. The diced carambolas give the sauce flavor while the remaining slices act as a garnish. To serve, divide the fish into 6 portions and place on individual plates. Spoon the sauce over the top.

6 servings.

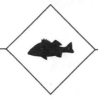

Lime-Baked Fish

An abundance of limes throughout the Keys leads to their use in many dishes. This simple recipe is a natural for any type of white fish fillets. Florida is now the largest U.S. producer of Persian limes—the limes that most of us know as just limes. The word "lime" is thought to come from the Arabic word "limah"; northern Europeans used limes to "cleanse the blood" at the end of winter. The acidity of limes acts as a flavor enhancer.

*2½ pounds yellowtail, dolphin, flounder, or cod
  fillets
3 sprigs fresh basil leaves, cut into small pieces
6 scallions, washed and thinly sliced*

*½ cup dry white wine
3 tablespoons unsalted butter
Grated zest of 4 to 6 limes
¾ cup fresh lime juice*

Preheat oven to 450 degrees. Cut a piece of aluminum foil large enough to completely envelop the fillets. Grease the foil and place on a baking sheet with edges turned up to contain the juices. Lay the fillets on one half of the foil and cover with the remaining ingredients. Fold the foil to cover the fish and seal the edges by pressing them together. Place baking sheet in oven and bake fish for 5 to 8 minutes or until the fish is just cooked; the flesh should be opaque rather than translucent.

6 servings.

SNOOK

The snook's mangrove habitat is being slowly destroyed, with a consequent decline in its population. This, coupled with its popularity, led to a fear that it would be overfished. Snook now has game-fish status. It has a delicious flavor and texture, something like that of snapper. Although snook can grow to about 50 pounds, the small ones of 1 to 2 pounds make the best eating.

Billy Knowles's Grilled Snook

Sit on the deck at the Cabana Bar at the Lorelei Restaurant in Islamorada about four in the afternoon. You'll see the bone fishermen returning and hear them tell their tales of fish lost and caught. They all look rugged and content, men who are doing something they love every day of their lives. Billy Knowles, a fourth-generation Conch, is one of the guides that everyone knows. His family originally came to Islamorada from the Bahamas in the late 1800's to farm pineapples. They shipped them up and down the Keys. With the demise of the pineapple plantations, Billy's father started fishing.

Any type of filleted white fish can be grilled in this way. The natural flavors and juices of the fresh fish are locked into the foil packet as it is grilled.

2½ pounds snook fillets
1 large onion, sliced
2 tablespoons butter

2 cloves garlic, crushed
2 tablespoons lemon juice
salt and freshly ground pepper to taste

Preheat the grill. Rinse the fillets and place on a large piece of foil. Arrange the sliced onion on top and dot with the butter and garlic. Sprinkle with lemon juice, salt, and pepper. Wrap the foil around the fish and place it on the grill. Allow 10 minutes per inch of thickness on a hot grill, and measure the fillets at their thickest point. Turn the fish packet several times while cooking. Check the fish by opening the foil and sticking the point of a knife into the meat. If it is opaque, it is done. Cut the fish into 6 portions and serve with the onion and juices spooned over the fish.

6 servings.

STINGRAY

Most rays that are used for food weigh 8 to 10 pounds. The terms "skate" and "ray" are used interchangeably. Stingrays are flat-bodied with fins that look like wings and a thin whiplike tail. They are bottom dwellers. The wing flesh, which is the edible portion of the fish, is firm and white, and it is often cut into small circles that resemble scallops in texture and flavor. Fishermen in the Keys are always skeptical when they see scallops on the menu. They're expensive to bring in and fish such as ray can be easily substituted. Ray will hold in the refrigerator 48 to 72 hours. The texture will become firmer as it "ages."

Sautéed Stingray

Eddie Wightman cuts his ray into steaks and skins and marinates them overnight. Dip your ray in bread crumbs and fry it, or try this lightly sautéed stingray.

1½ pounds skate	*1 lime or lemon, grated rind and juiced*
½ cup lemon juice	*2 tablespoons chopped chives*
½ cup unsalted butter (1 stick)	*salt and pepper to taste*

Wash stingray under running water. Scrub with a brush to remove thick coating. Divide wings into 6-ounce portions. Place pieces in a sautéing pan with straight sides in water to cover and add the lemon juice. Simmer gently for 15 minutes. Drain and place on a warm serving dish; cover. Heat the butter in a small saucepan to foaming; add the lime juice, half of the grated rind, and half of the chives. As soon as the butter starts to brown, pour it over the fish and sprinkle on the remaining grated rind and chives. Season with salt and freshly ground black pepper.

4 servings.

SEA TROUT (SPOTTED WEAKFISH)

Although it looks like a trout with bold black spots, the spotted sea trout is not related to fresh water trouts. It is a member of the weakfish family and is also called a spotted weakfish. The fish must be iced as soon as it is caught to retain its delicate texture and flavor.

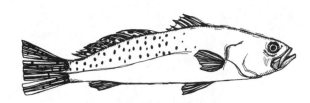

Susan Ellis's Sautéed Sea Trout

Gary Ellis combined his love and knowledge of bonefishing with his personal interest in finding a cure for cystic fibrosis. He started "The Redbone," Islamorada's Redfish/Bonefish All Release Celebrity Tournament. The funds raised go to help find a cure for cystic fibrosis and to help the children with this disease go to summer camps.

After a day out on the flats as a backcountry guide looking for bonefish, Gary stops on the way in to fish for dinner. He usually catches a couple of sea trout. He brings them home, fillets them, and gives them to his wife, Susan, to cook. Fish this fresh and good needs only a little cooking and a light sauce. Any light white fish such as flounder can also be used.

Look for some Redbone chardonnay to complete your meal. Bellevedere Winery in Sonoma Valley produces a private-label chardonnay for the tournament each year. Millard Wells, a well-known Keys artist, donates a painting as the first prize at the tournament. This is also used as the label for the Redbone chardonnay.

8 sea trout fillets
4 tablespoons unsalted butter (½ stick)
1 cup white wine

⅓ cup chopped fresh parsley
salt and freshly ground pepper to taste
1 tablespoon lemon juice

Wash and dry the fillets. Melt the butter in a skillet just large enough to hold the fish in one layer. When the butter is sizzling, add the fillets and sauté 2 minutes. Turn and sauté an additional 4 to 5 minutes. Poke the fillets with a pointed knife; if the flesh is opaque in the center, it is done. Remember the fish will continue to cook in its own heat when removed from the pan, so don't overcook it. Remove the fillets to a warm plate and cover with foil to keep warm. Add the wine to the pan and scrape up the brown bits. Cook over high heat to reduce by half. Add the parsley and salt and pepper to taste. Serve the fish sprinkled with lemon juice and with the pan sauces spooned over it.

4 servings.

WAHOO

The wahoo, a member of the mackerel family, resembles king mackerel and is considered the gourmet's mackerel. The flesh is white and delicately textured and is leaner than that of the king mackerel. It is scarce and difficult to find. King mackerel, commonly known as kingfish, can be substituted for wahoo.

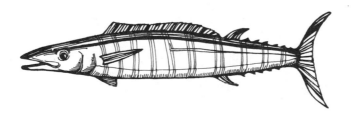

Grilled Wahoo with Papaya Salsa and Cilantro Butter—The Pier House

At The Pier House, Michael Kulow, executive chef, serves this spicy papaya salsa with his grilled wahoo to create a delicious taste sensation. The salsa can be made two days ahead and used as a garnish with any type of fish or chicken. The cilantro butter and the fish should be made just before serving.

◆

Papaya Salsa

1 small ripe papaya, coarsely chopped
1 ripe tomato, finely chopped
1 jalapeño pepper, seeded and coarsely chopped
½ red onion, finely chopped
1–1½ cups chopped cilantro
½ cup red wine vinegar

¼ cup olive oil
1 teaspoon ground cumin
½ tablespoon sugar
½ teaspoon Tabasco
salt to taste

Combine the ingredients in a medium bowl. Taste for seasoning and add more salt, cumin, or sugar as needed. Refrigerate for up to 2 days. Drain before serving.

◆

Cilantro Butter

½ cup coarsely chopped cilantro stems
½ cup white wine
3 tablespoons rice vinegar
1 bay leaf

4 black peppercorns
2 teaspoons sugar
1 cup heavy cream
4 tablespoons cold unsalted butter (½ stick)

Place the ingredients, except the cream and butter, in a saucepan and reduce until almost dry. Add cream and reduce by half. Remove from the heat and whisk in the butter one piece at a time. This will allow the sauce to retain its temperature and for the butter to thicken it. Strain and serve with the fish.

Makes about ¾ cup sauce.

◆
Cooking and Serving

6 6-ounce fillets wahoo or other light fish *salt and pepper to taste*
2 tablespoons olive oil

Prepare a charcoal or gas grill or preheat a broiler about 10 minutes before cooking. Brush the fish with the olive oil and sprinkle lightly with salt and pepper. Grill or broil 8 minutes for a 1-inch-thick fillet. Serve the fish with a little of the sauce spooned over it and the salsa as a garnish.

6 servings.

TUNA

Tuna are members of the mackerel family, but their taste is very different from that of mackerel. In fact, even among the many species of tuna the taste can vary considerably. The yellowfin and blackfin tuna are more delicately flavored and worth searching out; they work well with the recipes in Keys cuisine. Yellowfin and blackfin can be found in local fish markets in the Keys or can be bought from local fishermen at the end of their fishing day. I find the dark-meat bonito too strong tasting and prefer not to use it. Be sure to use tuna that is as fresh as possible in these recipes.

Tuna with Tangerine Coulis

Norman Van Aken mixes colorful bell peppers and tangerines together to make a bright and sunny garnish for grilled tuna.

◆

Tangerine Coulis

½ green pepper
½ yellow pepper
½ red pepper

1 cup tangerine juice
6 tablespoons balsamic vinegar

Place the peppers, skin side up, under the broiler until the skins begin to blacken. Remove the skins under running water and slice into very thin strips. Mix the tangerine juice and balsamic vinegar in a small saucepan. Reduce by half. Place the peppers in a small bowl and pour the reduced sauce over them. Mix well.

◆

Tuna Marinade

Tangerine Coulis
6 7-ounce slices yellowfin tuna
1 cup oil (safflower or corn)
½ cup olive oil
½ cup soy sauce
⅓ cup orange juice

¼ cup lemon juice
2 tablespoons lime juice
1 small bunch fresh cilantro
6 black peppercorns
2 bay leaves
2 large cloves garlic, halved

Prepare the Tangerine Coulis first. Then place the tuna in a baking dish. Mix the remaining ingredients and pour over the tuna; marinate for 5 minutes.

◆

Cooking and Serving

Preheat the grill or broiler. Drain the tuna and grill over medium heat for 10 minutes to medium-rare. Place the tuna on warmed individual plates and serve with the Coulis spooned over the top.

6 servings.

Norman Van Aken's Grilled Gingered Tuna with Black Bean Relish

Oriental spices and a Cuban Black Bean Relish make delicious accompaniments for this grilled tuna. Unusual flavor combinations are typical of Norman Van Aken's cooking.

There are several different types of tuna available. Yellowfin and blackfin tuna are considered the most desirable. Be sure the fish is as fresh as possible.

◆

Tuna Marinade

4 7- to 8-ounce tuna steaks
½ cup salad oil
¼ cup olive oil
¼ cup soy sauce
¼ cup orange juice
¼ cup lemon juice

¼ cup lime juice
1 small bunch cilantro, chopped
6 black peppercorns
2 bay leaves
2 large cloves garlic, halved

Place the tuna in a bowl. Combine the remaining ingredients and pour the marinade over the tuna. Marinate 10 to 15 minutes, turning once or twice.

◆

Cuban Black Bean Relish

2 cups cooked black beans*
½ cup sliced scallions (cut on an angle)
1 1-inch piece fresh ginger, finely chopped
¼ cup orange juice

¼ cup lime juice
¼ cup lemon juice
1 tablespoon sherry wine vinegar
salt and freshly ground black pepper to taste

Combine the beans, scallions, ginger, citrus juices, and vinegar in a saucepan. Warm gently over a low flame for 15 minutes, stirring occasionally. Taste for seasoning and add salt and pepper, as necessary.

*This step can be simplified by using canned black beans. Buy the best quality ones and rinse them thoroughly under cold running water. Or see Norman's Key West Shrimp (page 98) for his black bean recipe.

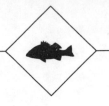

◆

Cooking and Serving

¾ cup orange segments

Preheat a grill or broiler, strain the tuna, and grill it until medium-rare. Depending on the thickness of the tuna, this will take about 5 minutes on the grill and about 8 minutes in the broiler.

Place the tuna on four individual plates, and spoon some black bean relish on top. Top the relish with orange segments. Serve immediately.

4 servings.

OTHER POPULAR GAME FISH

Here are some notes and information on other popular commercial and game fish.

Pompano Pompano, with its firm white flesh, is a delicacy. By baking the fish in its own packet, all of the natural juices are sealed in, and the fish gently steams. It may also be simply broiled and basted with a little butter.

Permit This fish is similar to pompano, but larger. Permits can be seen in the Keys, a hundred at a time, feeding in the shallows with their backs or tails out of the water. They are very shy, however, and difficult to catch. The best ones are 6 to 8 pounds; over that weight, they can be dry and coarse. They are excellent in chowders and poached.

Trunkfish or Boxfish Because their bodies are square, pentagonal, or nearly triangular, giving them a boxlike appearance, the various species of trunkfish are often called boxfish. Instead of scales, their heads and bodies are covered with a hard shell composed of rigid hexagonal plates. The boneless meat is similar to a chicken breast in texture, and is considered a delicacy. If a commercial fisherman catches one he usually keeps it for himself. The best way to enjoy boxfish is to stuff the inside and bake it in foil.

Cobia This is a large fish, weighing 30 to 50 pounds. Cobia are often mistaken for sharks because they stay near the surface and close to shore. They are game fish and also very good to eat. The meat is firm and white and good for cutting into chunks and deep-frying. They also smoke well. Cobia is sometimes served in restaurants in the Keys when a local fisherman shows up with a catch for sale.

Redfish or Red Drum Young drum fish, known as "puppy drums," usually weigh about 10 pounds and are caught mostly off the coast of Florida and in the Gulf of Mexico. Larger drum fish, weighing 20 to 30 pounds, are found off the coast of the Carolinas. Because drums can contain a trematode parasite, this fish should not be used in uncooked preparations such as ceviche, sashimi, or sushi. The parasite is killed during cooking, and the firm, heavy-flaked flesh is perfect for chowders.

Poultry and Meat Main Courses

Eden House Mango Chicken

Eden House, a quiet and sleepy little hotel on Fleming Street in Key West, may never be the same again. Goldie Hawn and a bevy of colleagues and movie equipment moved in to make a film that takes place in the sixties. Although having just completed a renovation of the hotel, Mike Eden agreed to turn the hotel back the way it was for the film. Rich's Cafe, in the Eden House, is owned and run by Diane Pansire. She was excited about serving the celebrities and cooked up this light, simple chicken dish made for the stars.

1 large ripe mango
1 ripe avocado
1 tablespoon butter or margarine
2 cloves garlic, crushed

2 teaspoons chopped fresh ginger
4 boneless, skinless chicken breasts, halved
salt and freshly ground black pepper to taste

Pit and peel the mango (see Glossary). Scrape out the flesh from the side sections. Puree the fruit in a food processor. Peel the avocado, cut in half, and remove the pit. Cut in quarters and make thin vertical slices nearly to the point in each quarter. Spread out like a fan and set aside. Melt the butter in a sauté pan and add the garlic, ginger, and chicken breasts. Brown the chicken on both sides, reduce the heat, and cook about 15 minutes or until the breasts are done. Add salt and pepper to taste. Spoon the pureed mango onto four individual plates and place one chicken breast on each plate. Garnish with the avocado and serve.

4 servings.

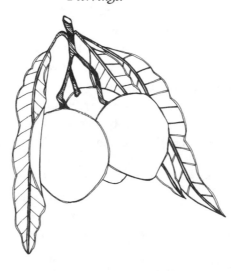

Banana-stuffed Chicken Breasts with Rum Sauce

When 11-year-old Dawn Sieber used to go fishing with her father in the Keys, they sometimes docked at Cheeca Lodge for Sunday brunch. Cheeca Lodge is a beautiful resort in Islamorada right on the ocean. She grew up and went to culinary college and fantasized about working at Cheeca. When Cheeca underwent its renovations two years ago, her father dared her to apply for a job. She took the dare and today is the executive chef at Cheeca. After owning a successful restaurant in Baltimore, she feels as if she has finally come home.

Banana, rum, and chayote are all tropical ingredients that Dawn enjoys using, and they are combined in this recipe. Chayote imparts a fresh taste to the garnish and has a slightly citrus tang when you bite into it.

◆

Chicken Breasts and Chayote

6 skinless boneless chicken breasts, halved
4 teaspoons salt
1 teaspoon freshly ground black pepper
1 teaspoon ground cinnamon
3 bananas, halved lengthwise
½ cup raisins

3 chayotes, peeled and sliced
2 tablespoons butter
2 teaspoons salt
½ teaspoon black pepper
½ teaspoon ground cinnamon

Place the chicken breasts on a cutting board, smooth side down. Flatten them with a meat mallet or the back of a skillet. They will be somewhat heart shaped. Mix the 4 teaspoons salt, 1 teaspoon pepper, and 1 teaspoon cinnamon and sprinkle a little on each flattened breast. Place a banana half on the point of the heart and sprinkle with a few raisins. Roll up the breast. Fill the other breasts in the same manner. Sprinkle the rolled breasts with any remaining cinnamon mixture and tightly wrap each one in plastic wrap. Bring a pot of water with a steaming rack to a boil and steam the wrapped chicken breasts, covered, for about 8 minutes. Remove to a plate and let cool a few minutes. Unwrap and slice on the diagonal into 2-inch pieces. Prepare the rice and the sauce.

Meanwhile, bring a second pot of water to a boil and add the chayote slices. When the water returns to a boil, drain the chayotes and rinse under running cold water. Melt the butter in a skillet and add the 2 teaspoons salt, ½ teaspoon pepper, and ½ teaspoon cinnamon. Over low heat, toss the chayote slices in the butter for about 4 minutes.

◆

Almond Rice

3 cups cooked rice (1½ cup uncooked)
½ cup blanched almonds, toasted
1 bunch scallions, washed and chopped

2 teaspoons salt
½ teaspoon pepper
½ teaspoon cinnamon

Mix the cooked rice with the almonds, scallions, and seasonings. Add more salt and pepper, to taste.

◆

Rum Sauce

2 tablespoons butter
3 shallots, chopped
½ medium onion, chopped
½ cup dark Myers's rum

2 tablespoons sugar
2 cups light cream
salt and freshly ground black pepper to taste

Melt the butter in a saucepan and add the shallots and onion. Sauté until transparent. Add the rum and sugar and let reduce by half. The sugar will dissolve and the sauce will become syrupy. Add the cream and reduce by half. Strain and season with salt and pepper.

◆

Serving

Place a large spoonful of rice in the center of each plate. Fan the chicken slices around three-quarters of the rice. Place the chayote slices in the remaining area. Spoon the sauce over the chicken and serve.

6 servings.

Keys Jerk Chicken

Spicy Caribbean food is becoming very popular in the United States. This Jamaican dish has found its way to the Keys over the years. Restaurants such as Sloppy Joe's on Duval Street serve Jerk Chicken. "Jerking" is an ancient Jamaican method for preserving and cooking meat. It is thought to have been invented by the Arawac Indians. Today the men who prepare the meat and sell it to the markets are called "jerk men." They use a long process, marinating the meat and then slowly cooking it over a pimento (allspice) wood fire. For this recipe I adopted the flavors and inspiration of jerk cooking. Helen Willensky, creator of Helen's Tropical Seasonings, helped me develop the generic Jerk Seasoning recipe. All of the ingredients can be found in supermarkets.

◆

Jerk Seasoning

2 tablespoons onion, chopped
4 teaspoons thyme, fresh or dried
4 teaspoons sugar

2 teaspoons salt
2 teaspoons ground nutmeg
2 teaspoons freshly ground black pepper

Chop the onion and mix with the seasonings. This can be done in a food processor or by hand. The juice from the onion will bind the other ingredients together. Set aside.

◆

Jerk Chicken

4 boneless, skinless chicken breasts, halved
2 tablespoons butter or margarine

1 tablespoon oil

Remove all fat from the chicken breasts and poke several holes in them. Spoon the Jerk Seasoning over both sides of the chicken and leave to marinate for 20 minutes.

Heat the butter and oil in a sauté pan and add the chicken. Gently sauté on each side for 5 to 10 minutes, depending on the size of the breasts. Serve with Pigeon Peas and Rice (see page 174).

4 servings.

Cuban Roast Chicken

Marinating the chickens overnight in sour-orange juice keeps them moist and flavorful during roasting. Many people use this same method for roasting their turkey to guarantee it will be tender and juicy.

2 3-pound chickens	*½ teaspoon black pepper*
8 cloves garlic	*1 cup sour-orange juice or ½ cup orange and*
1 teaspoon salt	*½ cup lime juice*

In each of the cavities of the two chickens, place 2 cloves garlic and a little salt and pepper. Truss the birds or at least tie their legs together. Crush the remaining cloves of garlic and mix with the sour-orange juice to make a marinade. Place the birds in a glass bowl or plastic bags with sealed tops and pour the marinade around them. Let them marinate overnight, turning a few times.

Preheat the oven to 400 degrees. Drain the chickens and place on a rack in a roasting pan. Roast for about 1 hour, basting several times with the marinade. Test to see that the chicken is done by piercing the thickest part of the thigh. If the juices run clear, the chicken is done. Another test is to push the drumstick, which should move easily in its socket. Remove the chickens from the oven. Cover them with foil and keep in a warm spot for 15 to 20 minutes before carving. Meanwhile, skim the fat off the pan juices and pour over the carved chicken.

6 to 8 servings.

Arroz con Pollo

Every Latin household and restaurant serves this flavorful and attractive dish. Before mass distribution of food supplies, everyone in the Keys had to depend on what they raised themselves or was attainable locally. Chicken and rice were always available. Many of the chickens were the raised-in-the-backyard variety. There are as many versions of this dish as there are people who make it. This one is very good and simple to make. It will also keep a day or two in the refrigerator and can be frozen. If you have Spanish olive oil, try it. It adds a slightly peppery flavor to the dish.

2 tablespoons olive oil
2 frying chickens, quartered or 8 pieces chicken
*   quarters*
salt and freshly ground black pepper to taste
1 large onion, diced
2 green peppers, diced
2 cloves garlic, crushed
1½ cups long grain rice

½ teaspoon saffron threads
3 cups chicken stock, heated
¼ cup dry sherry
4 fresh tomatoes, diced or 1 cup canned
*   crushed tomatoes*
½ cup tiny peas
½ cup green olives, pitted and quartered

Heat the oil in a skillet large enough to hold all of the chicken pieces in one layer, or use two skillets. Brown the chicken pieces, adding one piece at a time and moving it around until it starts to brown. When the oil is sizzling again, add another piece. This process allows the pan to regain the high temperature needed for browning, and moving the pieces as they go into the pan prevents them from sticking and burning. When all of the chicken is browned, remove to a plate and season with salt and pepper. Pour off any excess fat from the pan. Add the onions and sauté them until golden, about 10 minutes. Add the green pepper and garlic and sauté another 5 minutes. Add the rice and sauté 1 minute. Crush the saffron; soften in about 3 tablespoons of hot chicken stock and add to the rice. Add the remaining stock, sherry, and tomatoes to the pan. Stir well. Return the chicken to the pan, cover, and simmer for 20 minutes. Check the white meat by piercing the meat near the wing joint. If the juices run clear, the breasts are ready. Remove and cover with foil to keep warm. Add the peas and olives to the dark meat still in the pan and cook 10 minutes. Add salt and pepper to taste. To serve, spoon the rice onto individual plates or one large serving platter and top with the chicken pieces.

8 servings.

Edna Howard's Steam

Ninety-one-year-old Edna Howard entered the Cornish Memorial African Methodist Episco-pal (A.M.E.) Zion Church carrying fresh tomatoes from her garden for the busy kitchen. Edna was born and raised in Key West and married a Cuban. Her ancestors came from the Bahamas and helped to build the church. "There's no one left anymore who built this church," she told me. The tall white wooden church, which stands majestically over Whitehead Street in Key West, was first built in 1864 and has been reconstructed twice due to fire. Edna's cooking is a mixture of Bahamian, Conch, and Cuban, and she came that day to help out with the church lunches that were going out to offices in Key West. Fried Chicken or Barbecued Ribs, Yellow Rice or Macaroni and Cheese, and Baked Beans or Green Beans were on the menu.

Steam is a Conch word for stew and is one of the oldest recipes in the Keys repertoire. Edna gave me the recipe out of her head and it worked perfectly. She serves it with Yellow Rice (see page 175) and Fried Cabbage (see page 171)

2 pounds beef stew meat
1 tablespoon oil
1 28-ounce can tomatoes
¼ cup tomato paste
pinch of sugar

2 onions, chopped
1 green pepper, diced
4 large cloves garlic, crushed
salt and freshly ground black pepper to taste

Score the meat, place it in a pot of water, and boil until tender, about 1 hour. Drain the meat and pat dry with paper towels. Heat the oil in the same pan and brown the meat. Add the tomatoes and their juice, tomato paste, and sugar. Add water as necessary to cover the meat. Add the onions, green pepper, and garlic. Bring to a simmer and cook for about 30 minutes or until a sauce is formed. If the sauce looks thin, remove the meat and reduce the sauce over high heat to thicken it. Season with salt and pepper, to taste. Cut the meat into 2-inch pieces and return to the sauce for about 15 minutes. Serve meat and sauce together.

6 servings.

Bobbie's Bolichi

"My great grandfather would go around the neighborhood selling goat and cow's milk, and they always grew their own vegetables." Bobbie Sawyer grew up in Key West before the roads were improved and everyone had refrigeration. Bolichi is an old Cuban favorite. There wasn't a lot of meat available and this Cuban pot roast would last several days in her family. It's made with eye of round beef that has been stuffed with chorizo (spicy Cuban sausage) or boiled ham. Bobbie suggests asking your butcher to make the pocket for the stuffing. He will be able to make a hole through the center just large enough to hold the sausage. Otherwise, simply follow the directions in the recipe. This recipe calls for a whole head of garlic. In the slow cooking process, the garlic forms a puree and becomes a thickener.

3- to 5-pound beef eye of round
1 piece chorizo or other spicy sausage (as long as the length of the beef)
salt and freshly ground black pepper to taste
¼ cup flour
4 tablespoons olive oil
1 large onion, sliced

1 small green pepper, sliced
1 15-ounce can tomato sauce
1 cup water
2 teaspoons dried oregano
4 bay leaves
3 teaspoons paprika
1 head garlic, cloves crushed

Cut a hole in the meat and fit in the sausage. Season the meat with salt and pepper and dredge with flour. Add olive oil to a heavy-bottomed pan just large enough to hold the meat. Brown the meat. Add the rest of the ingredients. The water and sauce should come up about 3 inches in the pan. Be sure to stir the spices into the sauce. Bring the sauce to a boil. Cover and reduce to a simmer. Cook gently for 2½ to 3 hours, turning 2 or 3 times during the cooking. Check with a fork to see that the meat is tender. Remove the meat and stir the sauce. Slice the meat and return to the sauce for 5 minutes. Serve with rice and black beans.

8 servings.

Picadillo

According to Tim Duffy, manager of Sloppy Joe's Bar on Duval Street, picadillo is where the Sloppy Joe sandwich got its start. Picadillo, stewed ground meat, is served in almost every Latin restaurant, usually over rice or potatoes. Or, it can be served Sloppy Joe style over two halves of hollowed-out toasted Cuban bread. Olives and capers are always found in picadillo. Raisins are sometimes added for a slightly sweeter dish.

1 tablespoon olive oil
1 medium onion, chopped
4 cloves garlic, crushed
1 large green pepper, diced
2 pounds ground beef
2 cans 15-ounce tomato sauce

½ cup green olives, pitted and chopped
3 tablespoons capers
½ cup raisins (optional)
4 tablespoons Worcestershire sauce
4 tablespoons vinegar
salt and freshly ground black pepper to taste

Heat the oil in a skillet and add the onion. Sauté until the onion is golden, about 15 minutes. Add the garlic and green pepper and sauté gently 5 minutes. Add the beef, breaking it up into small pieces as it browns. Add the tomato sauce and mix well. Add the rest of the ingredients and stir until the meat is cooked through and flavors blended, about 15 minutes. Taste for seasoning, adding more vinegar and Worcestershire sauce if necessary.

8 servings.

Margaret Stevens's Jamaican Meat Pies—Lovin' Dough, Inc.

While traveling in Jamaica, Margaret Stevens discovered these Jamaican Meat Pies. She bought bags of them to take home and asked everyone she could for the recipe, but to no avail. In Margaret's words, "They're standoffish there." On her way to the airport, Margaret met a particularly friendly woman cab driver whom she convinced to give her the recipe. She's been selling them ever since from her little shop in Holiday Isle. They're great for picnics, lunch, or a light supper. Eat them hot or cold, or serve them with a piece of cheese melted on top. The pies freeze well. Baked, they will keep 24 hours in the refrigerator. Make small ones for hors d'oeuvres or to serve as appetizers.

I have adapted the recipe slightly and given you an easy pie dough to use. If you are pressed for time, use ready-made pie dough, puff pastry, or phyllo leaves found in the frozen food section of most supermarkets.

1 tablespoon oil
1 medium onion, chopped
2 green peppers, chopped
2 cloves garlic, crushed
1 pound ground beef chuck
1 cup tomato sauce
1 tablespoon tomato puree
1 teaspoon Tabasco sauce

2 teaspoons curry powder plus additional for
* sprinkling*
1 cup cold mashed potatoes (leftover or boiled
* and mashed)*
salt and freshly ground black pepper to taste
½ pound short crust pastry
1 egg
1 tablespoon water

Heat the oil in a large saucepan. Add the onion, peppers, and garlic and sauté until the onions are transparent but not browned, about 10 minutes. Add the ground meat and sauté until browned. Add the tomato sauce and puree and the Tabasco sauce; simmer for 10 minutes. Add the curry powder to the potatoes and stir the potatoes into the sauce to thicken it. Add salt and pepper. Taste the sauce and correct seasonings, if needed. Leave to cool.

Preheat oven to 350 degrees. Roll out the dough and cut into 4-inch squares. Mix the egg and water together and brush on the edges of each square. Place 1 to 2 tablespoons filling off center on each square. Fold the dough to form a triangle and press the edges to seal; brush each pie with egg wash and sprinkle with additional curry powder. Place on a baking sheet and bake 45 minutes or until the dough is golden brown.

Makes 24 meat pies.

◆
Short Crust Pastry

1½ cup all-purpose flour
1 teaspoon salt (optional)
6 tablespoons butter

2 tablespoons shortening
¼ cup ice water

Sift the flour and salt together into a bowl. Cut the butter and shortening into the flour, using a pastry blender or 2 knives, scissor-fashion, until the mixture resembles bread crumbs. Make a well in the center of the mixture and add 1 tablespoon water. Mix with a fork, adding more water to the drier areas as needed. When the mixture starts to come together in a ball, knead it lightly with your hands. Wrap in a plastic bag and place in the refrigerator to rest for at least 30 minutes. Use as directed.

Makes about 10 ounces pastry.

Manny and Isa's Cuban Pork Roast

Roast pork is a staple of Cuban cuisine. At their small restaurant in Islamorada, Manny and Isa add cumin to their basting sauce, which gives the pork an unusual flavor. They use it for their delicious Cuban Sandwiches.

3-pound boneless pork leg or pork loin roast
6 cloves garlic, crushed
½ cup lime juice

2 teaspoons cumin
1 teaspoon salt

With the point of a knife make small slits all around the pork. Combine the remaining ingredients in a bowl. Rub the marinade into the pork and let sit at least 1 hour or preferably overnight. Alternatively, simply place the pork in a plastic bag with a sealed top and pour in the marinade. Remove the pork from the marinade, place in a roasting pan and roast in a preheated 350-degree oven for 3 hours. Remove roast from oven and let stand, covered with foil, about 20 minutes. Slice and serve warm, let cool and slice for a cold meat platter, or use in Manny and Isa's Cuban Sandwiches (see page 182).

6 servings.

Barbecued Ribs

Barbecuing is a way of life in the Keys. There's always a breeze coming off the water, especially in the early evening, and it's a perfect setting for cooking and eating outdoors. Everyone has his or her own favorite barbecue sauce. I like this one because it uses orange juice as its base rather than tomato sauce. I find that tomato burns easily on a barbecue. This sauce gives the ribs a light, tangy flavor and is an interesting change from the more popular sweet barbecue sauces. It can be used for ribs or chicken pieces.

4 pounds baby back or pork loin ribs, cut into
 2-rib servings
¾ cup orange juice
¼ cup cider vinegar
2 chili peppers, seeded and chopped

6 cloves garlic, crushed
3 tablespoons Worcestershire sauce
3 tablespoons honey
1 teaspoon dry mustard

Score the ribs and place them in a baking dish or a plastic bag with a sealed top. Combine the remaining ingredients in a bowl and taste for seasoning, adding more mustard, Worcestershire, or honey as needed. Add more chili peppers if you like hot sauce. Pour the sauce over the ribs and let them marinate at least 2 hours or preferably overnight. Drain, reserving the sauce, and place the ribs on a preheated medium grill. Grill baby back ribs 30 minutes, basting once or twice; add another 15 to 20 minutes for larger ribs. To bake in the oven, place the ribs in a roasting pan and pour half the sauce over them. Bake in a preheated 350-degree oven for 1 hour or until the ribs are brown. Baste frequently. Pour the rest of the sauce over them and bake for 30 minutes more.

6 servings.

Mary Spottswood's Party Ham

Seven generations of Spottswoods have lived in Key West. When Mary married John Spottswood in 1949, he was a fifth-generation Conch. Now Mary and John's grandchildren are thriving. Their line goes back to the Maloneys and Barthlums, families involved in sponging, boating, politics, and real estate.

Mary learned how to bake ham from Manda Johnson, who worked for the Spottswood family, raised John Spottswood, and in turn his children. Everyone looked forward to Manda's ham at the Spottswood parties. Manda used to cook the ham in a brown paper bag. For safety's sake, Mary uses foil and puts the ham on when she goes to bed. She finishes it in the morning.

1 20-pound smoked ham with bone　　*1 cup brown sugar*
1 cup honey　　*1 cup maple syrup*
2 teaspoons ground cloves　　*1 cup mustard*
2 quarts apple juice

Line a roasting pan with foil and place the ham in it fat side up. Spoon the honey over the ham, sprinkle with ground cloves, and pour the apple juice over it. Loosely wrap the foil around the ham, forming a tent. Place in the oven and set the heat at 225 degrees. Bake for about 8 hours or overnight. Remove the skin and fat and score the meat in a diamond pattern. Spoon a little more honey over the top of the ham and add some more ground cloves. Let cook uncovered for 1 hour until it turns brown and a meat thermometer registers 160 degrees.

Combine the brown sugar, maple syrup, and mustard in a heavy-bottomed pan. Heat until the sugar dissolves and the sauce is thick. To serve, remove the ham from the pan and drain off all of the juices. Place on a serving platter and spoon some sauce over the ham. Slice the ham and serve the rest of the sauce on the side for dipping.

40 servings.

Roast Whole Pig

Roasting a whole pig is associated with large Latin parties or holidays. Every Saturday, B's Restaurant roasts a whole pig. They marinate the pig for 24 hours in a mixture of sour orange, garlic, mojo, and oregano. Bertha's uncle made the special box the pig is roasted in. It is lined inside with aluminum and a tray of aluminum fits across the top. A marinated 50-pound pig is placed in the box and the tray is placed over the top. A charcoal fire is built in the tray. The pig roasts from the top for 2 hours on one side and then is turned over and roasted for 2 more hours. An intense heat is produced by roasting in this special box, and the whole roast pig is done in about 4 hours. The pig will feed 50 to 60 people. It is served with moros y cristianos, a mixture of white rice and black beans.

SALADS, SIDE DISHES, AND SANDWICHES

Salads and side dishes are generally used as accompaniments. However, they make light meals on their own and are grouped here with sandwiches to complete your choices for luncheons or light meals.

Many Keys restaurants serve a simple green or mixed salad with their meals instead of a cooked vegetable, and dress it up with their special house dressing. The Pier House Hibiscus Dressing or Manny and Isa's House Dressing will make any salad seem special. Or if you like, try André Mueller's Salad Trevisana, which Mueller served to President Bush when the President was fishing in the Keys.

There are as many versions of conch salad as there are people who make it. I have included three examples that are really very different. Ziggie's Conch Salad marinates for at least 8 hours, giving the flavors a chance to blend. Monte's Conch Salad mixes the vegetables and conch with the sauce at the last minute, giving the salad a crunchy texture and fresh taste. The miso sauce in the Japanese Conch Salad adds another dimension to the salad. Try all three and serve each with enough bread to sop up the sauce.

Hearts of palm have been used as an exotic salad ingredient in many cuisines. In the Keys this vegetable is also known as Swamp Cabbage, which gives it a local character. Fresh hearts of palm are becoming more widely available now, but the canned ones are good and can be used in these recipes.

Usually either fried or baked potatoes accompany the main course. More recently, some tropical vegetables such as boniato, chayote squash, and malanga are becoming popular as side dishes. Try these unusual recipes to complete your menus.

Salads

Ziggie's Conch Salad

Conch salad is a Keys classic. Every restaurant or household has its own version. Henri Champagne, the chef at Ziggie's, marinates this salad overnight, and the result is a delicious blend of flavors.

2½ pounds conch
2 green peppers, diced
1 red pepper, diced
1 yellow pepper, diced (or use a second red
*   pepper)*
½ large onion, diced
6 tablespoons lemon juice

¾ cup sugar
3 tablespoons white vinegar
6 tablespoons oil
1 tablespoon water
5 or 6 drops Tabasco sauce
3 or 4 drops Maggi liquid seasoning

Rinse the conch and cut off the orange fin and foot and discard. Cut the conch into ½-inch chunks. Toss with diced peppers and onion. Combine the remaining ingredients and add salt and pepper to taste. Toss with the conch and vegetables. Marinate for 8 hours or overnight.

6 to 8 servings.

Monte's Conch Salad

Driving south toward Key West, in Summerland, you come upon Monte's Seafood. This small hut, with its large screened porch, belies the wonders that are inside. Mike Montalto places a major emphasis on finding the freshest fish possible. He has a special supplier for his Key West shrimp and knows just how to pick out the best conch. Everything is fresh here. You can't smell any fish when you walk in the door.

His conch salad is especially good. It is made fresh every day, and they pour the dressing over each individual salad just before it is served.

1½ pounds conch
½ green pepper, diced
½ red pepper, diced
½ cucumber, diced
2 stalks celery, diced
½ bunch scallions, diced
2 tablespoons white vinegar

¼ cup oil
1 bunch fresh basil, chopped
2 teaspoons dried oregano
2 cloves garlic, crushed
a few drops Tabasco sauce
sprinkling Old Bay

Rinse the conch and cut off the orange fin and foot and discard. Dice the conch and place in a bowl with the vegetables. Combine the remaining ingredients and beat well. Pour the dressing over the salad and sprinkle with Old Bay seasoning just before serving.

6 to 8 servings.

Japanese Conch Salad with Miso Sauce

Kyushu in Key West seems an unlikely place to look for Keys food, but it typifies the creative cuisine inspired by this mixture of cultures and blend of cooking styles. The French owner and Japanese chef use Keys ingredients to make Japanese dishes. In this salad, the conch is cut into thin, flat slices to look like a fan, and is then served with a sweet miso sauce.

2 whole conchs (about 1 pound each)	*¼ cup rice vinegar*
1 cucumber	*1 tablespoon water*
6-inch piece daikon radish	*2 teaspoons sugar*
1 box bean sprouts	*1 teaspoon dry mustard*

Rinse the conch, cut off the orange fin and the foot and discard. Place the conch in the freezer for about 1 hour so that it will be firm enough to slice thinly. Make several lateral slices of conch, following the shape of the fish, so that you are left with fan-shaped slices. The conch will be lying flat on the countertop. You slice parallel with the counter through the entire fish. You should get at least 4 thin slices from each conch. Tenderize the conch by taking the point of a knife and poking the slices until they are completely pockmarked. Peel and seed the cucumber and cut into thin slivers. Peel the radish and cut into thin strips. Wash and dry the bean sprouts. Place the vinegar, water, sugar, and mustard in a blender container and blend until smooth.

Rest the conch slices against the edge of a serving bowl to form a fan. Sprinkle the sprouts in the bottom of the bowl. Place the cucumber and radish on top of the sprouts and spoon a little sauce over the vegetables. Serve the rest of the sauce on the side for dipping. Serve immediately.

6 servings.

Monte's Shrimp Salad

At Monte's Seafood in Summerland the shrimp are big and pink. Lori Ann Pilotti makes a delicious salad using these treasures from the sea. The secret, of course, is the quality and freshness of the shrimp, but cooking them properly is essential.

2 pounds shrimp
5 stalks celery, diced
1 teaspoon fresh lemon juice

1½ cups mayonnaise
salt and freshly ground black pepper to taste

Rinse the shrimp and place in a steamer. Steam for 2 to 3 minutes only. Place immediately in ice-cold water. The meat will then easily separate from the shells. Peel and dice in ¼-inch cubes. Toss the shrimp and celery with the lemon juice. Combine with half of the mayonnaise, adding additional mayonnaise until the salad just holds together; don't overpower it with mayonnaise. Serve as a salad.

It also makes a delicious sandwich filling: Place some of the mixture on a sesame bun with lettuce, tomato, and a sprinkling of Old Bay seasoning.

8 servings.

Fresh Tuna Salad

The screen door opens right onto the docks at the Waterfront Fish Market in Key West. Charlene Borck, the owner, loves to cook and this is evident in her prepared-food display. Kathy Lewis who works with Charlene makes a delicious fresh tuna salad. Tasting a salad from fresh tuna rather than canned is a treat. In fact, whenever I serve broiled or grilled tuna and have leftovers, I make a salad for the next day. Fresh tuna is available in most fish markets. Here is Kathy's Fresh Tuna Salad.

2 pounds fresh yellow fin tuna	*1 medium onion, finely chopped*
2 bay leaves	*¼ cup chopped fresh parsley*
1 tablespoon Old Bay seasoning	*¼ cup sweet pickle relish*
1 cup mayonnaise	*1 teaspoon sugar*
2 hard-cooked eggs, coarsely chopped (optional)	*1 teaspoon lime juice*
2 stalks celery, diced	*salt and freshly ground black pepper to taste*

Place the tuna in a saucepan with water to cover. Add the bay leaves and Old Bay seasoning. Bring to a simmer and simmer gently until the tuna turns opaque or white, about 3 to 5 minutes. Drain and pat dry. Flake the tuna and mix with the rest of the ingredients. Taste for seasoning, adding salt and pepper as necessary.

6 to 8 servings.

Fresh Swamp Cabbage Salad

This interesting vegetable has two names. Call it swamp cabbage and it connotes down-home cooking. Use its other name, hearts of palm, and it could be served at the Ritz. If you are lucky enough to find fresh swamp cabbage, slice it thinly and soak in ice water for about 1 hour. Drain and serve with French Dressing or mayonnaise.

Ziggie's Hearts of Palm and Avocado Salad

This is a substantial salad. Serve it as a first course, salad plate, or light luncheon dish.

⅓ cup red wine vinegar
1 tablespoon spicy brown prepared mustard
1 tablespoon Dijon mustard
1 tablespoon water
½ cup corn oil
½ teaspoon oregano
½ teaspoon salt
½ teaspoon white pepper
½ teaspoon lemon juice

1 14-ounce can hearts of palm
4 avocados
*2 or 3 chicory or other lettuce leaves, washed
    and dried*
2 slices bacon, cooked and crumbled
3 tablespoons chopped black and green olives
¼ cup chopped pimento
½ cup seasoned croutons

To prepare dressing, whisk together the red wine vinegar, two mustards, and water. Mix well. Add the oil a little at a time, whisking constantly to incorporate it. Whisk in the oregano, salt, pepper, and lemon juice and taste for seasoning.

Slice the hearts of palm into thin rounds. Peel the avocados, cut in half, and remove the seeds. Place each half round side up on a cutting board and cut thin slices from the round end to the point, being careful not to cut through the point. Arrange a bed of chicory leaves on each of 8 individual plates and sprinkle with the sliced hearts of palm. Place an avocado half on top of each, fanning out the slices. Spoon dressing over top and serve sprinkled with bacon, olives, pimentos, and croutons.

8 servings.

Salad Trevisana with Dill-Chive Dressing

André Mueller, chef de cuisine of Marker 88, made this salad as part of the presidential dinner for President Bush's April 21, 1990, fishing trip to Islamorada.

Trevisana is a small town in Northern Italy where radicchio is grown. The dressing should be very thin and light.

1 head Boston lettuce
¼ pound fresh baby spinach
1 medium head radicchio
2 endive
1 bunch watercress
1 egg yolk
1 teaspoon prepared mustard

3 tablespoons red wine vinegar
¾ cup corn oil
¾ cup half-and-half
1 cup snipped fresh chives
1 cup snipped fresh dill
1 teaspoon sugar
salt and freshly ground white pepper to taste

Wash and dry all of the greens and tear into bite-sized pieces. Place on 6 individual salad dishes. Whisk the egg yolk in a small bowl until thick and add the mustard and vinegar. Continue whisking and add the oil drop by drop. When the dressing is thick, slowly add the cream. The dressing should be smooth and thin. Add the herbs, sugar, and salt and pepper to taste. Spoon some dressing over the salad and serve the rest on the side.

6 servings.

Manny and Isa's Coleslaw

Manny and Isa make their coleslaw with pineapple and vinegar, which gives it a sweet-and-sour flavor.

9 cups shredded cabbage (about 1 small head)
1 cup grated carrot
1 tablespoon white vinegar
¼ cup sugar

*1 20-ounce can chopped, crushed unsweetened
pineapple, drained*
1½ cups mayonnaise
1 teaspoon white pepper
1 teaspoon salt

Place the cabbage and carrot in a large bowl and toss with vinegar and sugar. Add the pineapple. Mix in half of the mayonnaise, adding just enough more to barely hold the coleslaw together. Taste for seasoning. Add salt and pepper if necessary. Serve as side dish.

8 servings.

Tropical Coleslaw

Coleslaw is served in nearly every restaurant in the Keys. Pink grapefruit and Key lime juice add a tropical tang to this version. The salad tastes best when marinated an hour or more before serving. This recipe is easy to make if you have a food processor fitted with a slicing blade. If not, slice the vegetables by hand.

½ head green cabbage, washed and drained
2 carrots, peeled and washed
1 small onion
2 tablespoons corn oil
2 pink grapefruits

2 tablespoons Key lime juice (lime juice may
* be substituted)*
4 teaspoons sugar
4 tablespoons mayonnaise
2 teaspoons Dijon mustard
salt and freshly ground black pepper to taste

Thinly slice the cabbage, carrots, and onion. Place in a bowl and toss with oil. With a serrated stainless steel knife, peel the grapefruits, carefully removing the white pith. Working over the cabbage bowl, cut the grapefruits into sections, allowing them and the juice to drop into the bowl as they are cut. Mix in the lime juice and sugar. Add the mayonnaise and mustard and toss well. Add salt and pepper to taste. Toss again before serving.

6 servings.

Black Bean and Rice Salad

What do you do with leftover black beans and rice? Sally Thomas of Key West makes this quick and easy salad. The salad is so good that I don't wait for leftovers to make it. The cilantro gives this dish a wonderfully fresh taste.

*2 cups cooked or canned black beans (rinse
    and drain canned beans)
2 cups cooked rice
1½ cups fresh cilantro
¼ cup lime juice*

*¾ cup oil
½ cup chopped onion
2 cloves garlic, crushed
salt and freshly ground black pepper to taste*

Mix the beans, rice, and cilantro together in a bowl. Place the lime juice in a small bowl and whisk in the oil. Add the onion and garlic and toss with the rice and beans. Add salt and pepper to taste.

6 servings.

Manny and Isa's House Dressing

*⅓ cup white vinegar
⅓ cup water
3 cloves garlic
6 teaspoons sugar
1 teaspoon black pepper
1 teaspoon dried oregano*

*½ teaspoon ground nutmeg
½ cup spearmint leaves (any type of mint may
    be used)
1 egg white
½ cup vegetable oil*

Combine the ingredients, except the oil, in a blender container and mix. With the blender running, add the oil in a slow stream. Mix until the dressing is white and creamy. Toss with salad or serve on the side. This will dress 8 to 10 salads.

Makes about 1¼ cups.

The Pier House Hibiscus Vinaigrette

Hibiscus shrubs grow abundantly in this tropical region. Their bright flowers bloom for just one day. Michael Kulow uses hibiscus tea to flavor his vinaigrette sauce at the Pier House. Use it for any type of green salad.

1 hibiscus tea bag
¼ cup boiling water
¼ cup vegetable oil
¼ cup olive oil
⅓ cup raspberry vinegar

1 grated rind of orange
*4 ounces fresh raspberries**
2 teaspoons sugar
salt and white pepper to taste

Steep the hibiscus tea bag in the boiling water for 5 minutes. Remove the bag and reduce the tea by about half. Let cool. Whisk all of the ingredients together thoroughly. Taste for seasoning, adding more salt, pepper, or sugar as needed.

Makes about 1 cup.

*Frozen unsweetened raspberries can be substituted for fresh.

Side Dishes

Fried Cabbage

Edna Howard serves this fried cabbage with her Steam (see page 143) and Yellow Rice (see page 175).

½ *pound bacon*   *freshly ground black pepper to taste*
½ *head cabbage, cored and coarsely sliced*

Cut the bacon into 2-inch pieces. Sauté in a skillet until crisp. Drain on paper towels. Pour off all but a tablespoon or so of the fat and sauté the cabbage in it until soft. Toss the cabbage with the bacon and add pepper to taste. Serve with steam.

6 servings.

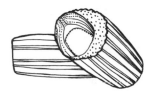

Cooked Swamp Cabbage

Here is an interesting side dish to complete one of your Keys dinners.

4 swamp cabbages, about 6 inches long and 2   *3 cups water*
  inches wide or two 14-ounce cans hearts of   *1 cup light cream*
  palm   *2 teaspoons black pepper*
½ *pound salt pork, cut into pieces*   *1 teaspoon salt*

Cut the swamp cabbage into ¼-inch pieces and mix the swamp cabbage, salt pork, and water in a saucepan. Bring to a rolling boil, reduce heat, and cook 1 hour. Add the cream and half of the salt and pepper. (Be careful; there may be enough salt from the pork.) Simmer another 5 minutes. Taste for seasoning.

4 servings.

St. James Missionary Sweet Potato Pie

Down the street from the Hemingway house in Key West is the St. James Missionary Baptist Church on Olivia Street. Rattling pans, laughter, and talking drew me to the back of the church, where I found several ladies at work in the kitchen. "Just call us friends of the Church," they said as they told me about their favorite dishes. Having come to this area in 1945 from "Carolina," their cooking has a distinct Southern flavor. Fried chicken, coated with self-rising flour, collard greens (made with ham hock and onions on the side, so they won't spoil the greens), and sweet potato pies are some of the foods they make and sell to raise funds. This particular week they were making their sweet potato pies on Saturday to sell for Sunday lunch. It was worth an extra trip back to the church to pick up my fresh, warm pie when it was ready.

Short Crust Pastry (see page 147)
2 cups cooked sweet potatoes (about 1¼ pounds
  potatoes)
2 tablespoons butter, softened
¼ cup sugar

¼ teaspoon ground nutmeg
½ teaspoon ground cinnamon
1 egg
¼ cup milk

Prepare the Short Crust Pastry and line an 8- to 9-inch pie plate. Peel potatoes and cut into cubes. Place in a pot of cold water, cover, and bring to a boil. Boil until soft, about 25 minutes. Drain, add butter, and mash well. Let cool before adding the egg. Mix in sugar, spices, egg, and milk. Spoon into pie shell and bake in a preheated 400-degree oven for 45 minutes. The pastry should be a light golden brown and the pie filling set. Slice and serve hot or cold. This dish freezes well.

8 servings.

Spiced Boniato

Tropical root vegetables are becoming better known in the Keys as well as throughout the United States. Their unusual flavors and textures are used more frequently in the new style of Keys cuisine that is appearing at many of the more creative restaurants. Boniato is a type of tropical sweet potato. It has a smooth texture when cooked, and is only slightly sweet. Try to buy small boniatos. They are tenderer than the large ones. Allspice comes from the berry of the allspice tree. The taste and aroma are suggestive of cinnamon, nutmeg, and cloves. The boniato develops an intriguing flavor when mixed with this spice. Sweet potatoes or yams may be substituted.

2 pounds boniatos
4 tablespoons butter or margarine (½ stick)

½ teaspoon allspice
salt and freshly ground black pepper to taste

Wash and peel the potatoes. Place in cold water as soon as they are peeled. Cut into pieces about the size of large marbles. Drop into a pot of boiling water, making sure the potatoes are completely covered with water. Boil for 15 to 20 minutes until soft. Heat the butter in a separate pan and add the allspice, salt, and pepper. Drain the potatoes and toss them in the spiced butter.

6 servings.

Boiled Malanga

Malanga is a tropical root vegetable and an important source of protein for many tropical cultures. It can be peeled and cooked like potatoes. Its cooked white flesh is slightly sweeter and nuttier in flavor than potatoes and can be served seasoned with just salt and pepper. Edna Howard at the Cornish Memorial AME Church serves malanga with her Steam (see page 143). She adds a sauce of garlic and onion to the malanga. "I used to pour hot lard over the mashed malanga, but now everyone's against lard and I can't do that anymore. It sure was good, though." Edna is a healthy and active 91.

*1½ pounds malanga, peeled and cut into
   chunks (3½ cups)
¾ cup butter (1½ sticks)*

*1 medium onion, sliced
6 cloves garlic, crushed
salt and freshly ground black pepper to taste*

Place the malanga in a pot of cold water, cover, and boil for 25 to 30 minutes or until soft. Meanwhile, melt the butter in a small skillet and add the onion and garlic. Cook until the onion is transparent. When the malanga is soft, drain and mash well. Beat in the onion and garlic sauce and season with salt and pepper to taste.

4 to 6 servings.

Pigeon Peas and Rice

Pigeon peas and rice is a well-known dish throughout the Caribbean. Pigeon peas are small, round legumes about the size of regular peas; they can be bought either frozen or canned. The recipe calls for cooking the rice and pigeon peas together. If you have leftover rice, use it instead. Cut the water by half and cook the rice and peas for 5 to 10 minutes to warm through.

*1 tablespoon oil
1 small onion, chopped
2 cloves garlic, crushed
6 tablespoons tomato sauce
1 16-ounce can pigeon peas*

*1 cup uncooked rice
4 tablespoons chopped fresh parsley
2 cups water
1 tablespoon fresh lime juice
salt and freshly ground black pepper to taste*

Heat the oil in a saucepan and add the onion; simmer for 5 minutes. Add the garlic and tomato sauce and cook 1 minute. Add the peas, rice, and parsley and sauté 1 minute. Add the water and lime juice and simmer, covered, for 15 minutes until rice is cooked. Add salt and pepper to taste.

4 servings.

Edna Howard's Yellow Rice

Rice is a staple in the Conch diet and yellow rice is a particular favorite. Edna Howard makes a yellow rice that is a cross between Bahamian Pigeon Peas and Rice and Cuban Yellow Rice. Bijol is a Latin spice made from ground annatto seed. It gives the food a yellow color. Tumeric may be used instead. Pigeon peas can be bought either frozen or canned.

¼ pound bacon, cut into 2-inch pieces
1 medium onion, sliced
2 cloves garlic, crushed
½ cup pigeon peas or lima beans, drained

1 cup long grain rice
2 cups water
1 teaspoon bijol
salt and freshly ground black pepper to taste

Sauté the bacon in a saucepan until translucent; pour off most of the fat. Add the onion and sauté until transparent. Add the garlic, peas, and rice and sauté several minutes. Add the water and bijol, cover, and simmer until the rice is cooked and the water is absorbed, about 20 minutes.

6 servings.

Fried Plantains

Fried Plantains, also called *patacones* and *tostones,* are served with almost any dish in Latin restaurants, whether it's fish, chicken, or pork. Plantains are large, green, and sometimes slightly bruised looking bananas. Peeling a plantain is a little tricky. The peel wants to stick to the flesh. Take a knife and slit the skin along the natural ridges of the fruit. Then peel the strips away. Yellow or slightly ripe plantains are best for this recipe. It can take about a week for green plantains to ripen at home. If you have a yellow plantain that is not quite ripe yet, place it in a 300-degree oven until it turns black and the skin begins to split; this only works with plantains that have already started turning yellow.

4 yellow plantains　　　　　　　　　　　　*salt to taste*
oil for frying

Peel and slice the plantains about 1 inch thick. Pour the oil into a pan for deep-frying and heat to 325 degrees. Slide the plantain slices in a few at a time and fry until golden. Drain on paper towels, then place on waxed paper. Cover with another piece of waxed paper and flatten the slices with a mallet or the bottom of a heavy skillet to about ¼ inch thick. Raise the temperature of the oil to 350 degrees and fry the flattened plantains until lightly browned. Drain on paper towels, sprinkle with salt, and serve.

6 servings.

Sandwiches

Harvey's Fish Sandwich

The Pilot House started out in the 1950's as a beer house with a pool table where all of the local fishermen congregated to drink beer and socialize. This area in the Keys was really a fishing community with some weekend people from Miami. In the seventies the pool table was removed and the restaurant started. The Pilot House looks out on Lake Largo and has a 29-slip marina and deep-water dockage. You can come by boat or car and soak up some of the Keys atmosphere. One of the most popular menu items at the Pilot House is Harvey's Fish Sandwich.

Harvey's story and his fish sandwich have become standard fare throughout the Upper Keys. As a retired, disabled fireman, Harvey came to the Keys and worked as a fish cutter at the Pilot House Restaurant in the seventies. Everyone knew Harvey with his khaki pants and shirt, no shoes, and ever-present bicycle. In those days, he cut fish fillets for 20 cents a pound and cheeks and throats for 2 cents a pound. Any leftover fish was his. With his fish, some onions, eggs, and bread, he would fry up a sandwich for himself. He lived at a nearby boat yard and started frying this sandwich in large pans for any of the stray fishermen who happened to be around. Soon, people were coming into the Pilot House asking for Harvey's Fish Sandwich. Craig Belcher, a chef at the Pilot House, developed Harvey's sandwich so that it could be made on a more commercial basis. Within six months, it became thirty percent of their business. Now it is the most copied sandwich in the Keys. Here is Craig's original version.

3 ounces grouper or dolphin fillets
2 tablespoons bread crumbs
oil for frying
1 tablespoon butter
½ cup diced onion

1 slice yellow cheese (any type)
2 slices whole wheat toast
1 tablespoon Tartar Sauce (page 180)
2 slices tomato

Roll the fish fillets in the bread crumbs. Heat the oil in a deep pan to 350 degrees and fry the fish for 3 to 4 minutes or until golden. In a skillet, melt butter and sauté onions until golden. Meanwhile, put a slice of cheese on each piece of toast and place in the oven to melt the cheese. (In the restaurant they place the bread on a large griddle or grill and melt the cheese on the bread.) To serve, place the fish fillets on a piece of the toast, cover with onions, add the tartar sauce and tomato slices, and cover with the second piece. Cut in half and serve immediately.

Makes 1 sandwich.

Garrison Bite Fish Sandwiches

Sitting on the Garrison Bite, you feel as if you are on your own boat looking out over Garrison Bight, Key West's municipal marina. The Bite is a floating restaurant, and you can order whatever they have for that day, or bring in your own fish and let Tom McCutchen, the owner and chef, cook it for you.

1½ pounds fresh fish fillets	*6 sesame rolls*
1 tablespoon lime juice	*6 lettuce leaves*
1 egg	*6 slices tomato*
1 12-ounce can beer	*6 slices onion*
1 cup all-purpose flour plus 2 tablespoons	*Tartar Sauce (recipe follows)*
oil for frying	

Sprinkle the fish with lime juice. Mix the egg, beer, and 1 cup flour in a bowl. Coat the fish with the remaining 2 tablespoons flour and then dip into the batter. Heat the oil in a deep fryer to 350 degrees. Fry the fillets for 1½ minutes. Drain and serve on a sesame roll with lettuce and tomato and onion slices. Serve tartar sauce on side.

Makes 6 sandwiches.

◆

Tartar Sauce

1 cup mayonnaise	*1 tablespoon lime juice*
3 tablespoons mustard	*1 teaspoon Worcestershire sauce*
1 tablespoon chopped onion	*salt and pepper to taste*
1 tablespoon sweet relish	

Combine the ingredients in a small bowl and add salt and pepper to taste.

Moon Fish Sandwich

Novelist Phil Caputo's 569-pound marlin caught off the coast of Cuba dominates one entire wall of the Full Moon Saloon on Simonton Street in Key West. The history of the Full Moon parallels the history of Key West in the late seventies and early eighties, when Key West was developing from a sleepy fishing village into a tourist haven. The Full Moon was home for fishermen, drug runners, and gunrunners—all with big thirsts and a desire to mingle with friends. They were a rough crowd. The fact that the clientele is a little more sophisticated today is an indication that Key West has changed. Yet, the bar is still filled with local color and characters.

One of the saloon's more famous menu items is their grouper sandwich. They serve it open-faced, with macaroni salad, lettuce, and tomato on the side.

¼ pound grouper fillet	*1 sesame roll*
1 teaspoon lime juice	*1 tablespoon butter*
1 egg	*¼ small onion, sliced*
1 tablespoon buttermilk	*4 mushrooms, sliced*
¼ cup beer	*1 slice cheddar cheese*
2 tablespoons flour	*1 tomato, cut into wedges*
2 tablespoons cracker meal	*lettuce*
oil for frying	*1 pickle, sliced*

Sprinkle the fish with lime juice. Combine the egg and buttermilk in one bowl and the beer, flour, and cracker meal in a second one. Dip the fish in egg wash and then batter. Heat the oil in deep fryer to 350 degrees and fry the fish for 3 to 4 minutes until golden brown. Open the roll and place fish on both halves.

Meanwhile, melt the butter in a skillet and sauté the onion until transparent. Add the mushrooms and continue to cook for several minutes. Place the mushrooms and onions on the fish and top with cheese. Place under the broiler to melt the cheese. Serve open-faced on platter with a garnish of pickle, tomato wedges, and lettuce.

Makes 1 sandwich.

Manny and Isa's Cuban Sandwiches

When in Islamorada, stop at Manny and Isa's restaurant for a delicious Cuban sandwich, which is not unlike the All-American Dagwood sandwich. The Cubans take their sandwich one step further by placing it under a hot sandwich press. (The press works on steam heat.) The sandwich becomes flattened while the ingredients are warmed through and the cheese just slightly melted. The treat about Manny and Isa's sandwiches is that they roast their own pork. The recipe is on page 147, but you can make a very good sandwich with good-quality store-bought cold cuts.

4 Cuban bread rolls, steak rolls, mini sandwich rolls, or submarine rolls	¼ pound salami, thinly sliced
4 tablespoons butter	¼ pound Swiss cheese, thinly sliced
4 tablespoons prepared mustard	¼ pound roast pork, thinly sliced
¼ pound boiled ham, thinly sliced	3 or 4 dill pickles

Cut the roll in half lengthwise. Generously spread butter on one side and mustard on the other. Cover the buttered side with a layer of ham, then a layer of salami, then a layer of cheese, and finally a layer of roast pork. Slice the pickles ¼ inch thick and place a row of pickle slices on the pork. Close the sandwich with the other half of the roll. Heat a sandwich press and place the sandwich in it for 2 to 3 minutes. Alternatively, place the sandwich on a baking tray, cover with foil, and place in a preheated 400-degree oven for 5 minutes. Serve with coleslaw and pickles.

Makes 4 sandwiches.

DESSERTS

Mention the Keys and Key limes come immediately to mind. This rugged little yellow lime has a varied and interesting history and merits a section all its own (see Glossary). Key Lime Pie, with all its variations, is the most renowned dessert of the Keys. In the days before refrigeration, sweetened condensed milk was the only milk available. It was natural to put it together with native Key limes to make a Key lime pie.

In addition to Key lime pie, I have developed or discovered an entire repertoire of Key lime recipes—Snook's Key Lime Cheesecake, Key Lime Chocolate Chip Ice Cream, Key Lime Sorbet, and Key Lime Coconut Cookies are a few of the tempting desserts made with this unique citrus. Over the past few years, citrus canker hampered the distribution of Key limes throughout the United States, but now Haitian Key limes are widely available and distributed year-round. Bottled Key lime juice is also available.

This section goes beyond Key limes to explore some delicious and interesting recipes using other tropical fruits grown in the Keys. Passion fruit, mangoes, coconut, and strawberries are all readily available. Passion Fruit Pie became my family's favorite dessert. From May to August ripe juicy mangoes hang lusciously from the trees just waiting to be picked. Mango Pudding, Ice Cream, and Sorbet are all delectable and easy to make. With tropical fruits becoming commonplace in most supermarkets, you can add an exotic touch to your repertoire. Queen of All Puddings makes a festive holiday dish, while Cuban Banana Rum Custard Tart brings a new meaning to banana pie. Piña Colada Cheesecake tastes as exotic as it sounds. To end, a collection of tea breads—avocado, passion fruit, strawberry, mango coconut, and Bimini—will tempt even nonbread bakers to turn their hand to produce these mouth-watering treats.

My popularity on the street where I live increased as my neighbors and friends joined me in taste-testing the recipes in this chapter. These recipes are full of flavor and fun, and I know you will enjoy them too.

Key Lime Desserts

Manny's Key Lime Pie

"This is the original Key Lime Pie," is a common claim in the Keys. As with any regional recipe that has evolved over the years, it is difficult to say what "an original" is. Joseph Sassine, chef at the Green Turtle Inn, says that the original pie had a short crust pastry and a thick layer of meringue on the top. The sheer volume of pies made today makes preparation of the crust and meringue too time-consuming for many restaurants. Pies with graham cracker crusts and whipped cream toppings are now more common.

Manny and Isa's small restaurant in Islamorada serves a wonderful "original" Key Lime Pie. They use Key limes from their own Key lime trees out back. The acid content of fresh Key limes causes the pie to set immediately. If you are using bottled Key lime juice or regular fresh lime juice, then the pie will need to sit in the refrigerator to set.

Short Crust Pastry (see page 147)
4 extra large eggs, separated
1 14-ounce can sweetened condensed milk

½ cup Key lime juice
¼ teaspoon cream of tartar
½ cup sugar

Prepare Short Crust Pastry as instructed. Preheat the oven to 375 degrees. Remove dough from the refrigerator, roll it out, and line a 10-inch pie plate. Place a piece of foil or waxed paper in the shell and fill with rice or dried beans. Place in the preheated oven for 10 minutes. Remove the filling and foil and return to the oven for 10 more minutes or until just golden. Cool.

Beat the egg yolks and condensed milk until creamy. Fold in the Key lime juice until the mixture thickens. Fill the baked pie shell with the mixture.

Preheat the oven to 375 degrees. Beat the egg whites to a medium peak. Add the cream of tartar and continue to beat. Slowly add the sugar and beat until the mixture is stiff. Spread the meringue over the pie, sealing it to the crust. Bake until golden brown, about 5 minutes.

8 to 10 servings.

Key Lime Tart La Croissanterie

Claude Lucas came to Key West in 1983 and opened his delightful Croissants de France on Duval Street. Sitting on his charming porch eating freshly made croissants, you might think you were on the Champs Elysées until you try some of his Key West creations. He has applied his expertise and inventiveness as a French pastry chef to Key West ingredients. One of the results is this Key Lime Tart.

Chocolate and Key lime juice go well together. If you love chocolate, a variation following this recipe calls for a chocolate coating over the crust before the filling is poured in.

1 baked 9-inch Sweet Pastry Crust shell (recipe follows)	4 tablespoons unsalted butter (½ stick)
1 cup fresh Key lime juice	7 eggs
1½ cups sugar	½ cup heavy cream (optional)

Prepare the Sweet Pastry Crust and bake as instructed.

Combine the Key lime juice, sugar, and butter in a heavy-bottomed saucepan and cook over low heat, stirring occasionally, until the sugar is dissolved. Do not let the mixture boil. Beat the eggs in a bowl; very slowly, stirring constantly to prevent curdling, pour in the lime juice mixture. Return the mixture to the pan and cook over low heat to thicken, stirring constantly. The filling is ready when the mixture coats the back of a spoon. (This means that when you draw your finger across the back of the stirring spoon, a definite line remains.) Remove from heat and continue to stir a few minutes until cool. Then pour into the prepared pie crust and refrigerate to set, about 30 minutes.

Whip the cream and pipe little rosettes all along the edge of the pie. If you are in a hurry, simply sprinkle some confectioners' sugar over the top just before serving.

8 servings.

◆

Sweet Pastry Crust

2 cups unsifted all-purpose flour
¼ cup walnuts, finely chopped
½ cup unsalted butter (1 stick), room
   temperature

½ cup sugar
3 egg yolks
1 teaspoon vanilla extract

Sift flour onto a working surface. Mix in the walnuts. Clear a wide circular space in the center of the flour and place the softened butter in it. Be careful not to let the butter touch the flour until the butter has been mixed with the other ingredients. With your fingers, make a little nest in the center of the butter. Put the sugar on top, the egg yolks on this, and the vanilla on top of the yolks. Using your fingers in a tapping motion, work the butter mixture until it is smooth. (Alternately, this can be done in a food processor.) When the mixture is smooth, incorporate the flour gradually and work until everything comes together in a ball. Place in a plastic bag and let rest in the freezer for 1 hour or refrigerate overnight.

Preheat oven to 325 degrees. Roll out the pastry and fill a 9- or 10-inch pie plate. Prick the surface of the crust all over with a fork and cover with parchment paper or foil. Fill the shell with rice or dried beans to weigh down the paper. Bake for 12 minutes. Take out of the oven and remove the rice and paper, saving the rice for the next time. Return the shell to the oven and continue baking another 8 to 10 minutes until the crust is a golden color but not brown. Let cool.

◆

Chocolate Key Lime Tart

2 ounces semisweet chocolate

¼ cup light cream

Combine the ingredients in a heavy-bottomed saucepan and cook over low heat until the chocolate is melted and the mixture smooth. Pour the mixture into the baked pie shell and refrigerate to harden. Prepare the filling for Key Lime Tart La Croissanterie (recipe precedes) and pour it into the chilled shell.

Eggless Key Lime Pie

Gardner's Markets is a chain of gourmet food stores that has had an outlet in North Key Largo since 1965. At that time, this area, now known as the Ocean Reef Club, was a boating and fishing village containing a small enclave of houses and a rustic little hotel. Many boaters pulled up to the dock at Gardner's to get their food supplies, and Joe Gardner himself sometimes brought supplies down from Miami by boat. Today, Elizabeth and Maurice Adams, third-generation Gardners, run the stores. Pam Manresa, who is in charge of Gardner's main commissary, developed this version of Key Lime Pie for Gardner's. Her objective was a pie that would not spoil in hot weather when a customer transported it from the store to his or her home. A pie without eggs was the answer.

1½ cups graham cracker crumbs *3 cups sweetened condensed milk*
¼ cup packed dark brown sugar *⅓ cup Key lime juice*
6 tablespoons unsalted butter (¾ stick), melted

Place the graham cracker crumbs and sugar in a bowl. Stir the melted butter into the crumbs and press the mixture into a 9- or 10-inch pie plate. Set aside.

Combine the condensed milk and Key lime juice in a bowl. Pour the filling into the pie crust. Cover well and refrigerate until ready to use. The pie can be frozen. Serve with a topping of whipped cream if you like.

8 to 10 servings.

Key Lime Fruit Tart

The inspiration for this recipe came from Linda Haywood's entry at the Island Jubilee Cook-Off held in Key Largo. Her pie looked like a French Fruit Tart, but the filling was flavored with Key lime juice rather than vanilla. The filling is easy to make and can be frozen. So make extra and freeze some for another pie or to fill some dessert crepes.

Dessert pies are enhanced by a sweet pastry, such as the Sweet Pastry Crust on page 191. It, too, can be made ahead and frozen. If pressed for time, however, use a ready-prepared pie crust.

The fruit for the topping should be colorful and ripe. I have given fruit suggestions. Choose what you are going to use according to availability. This tart makes an attractive party dessert.

Sweet Pastry Crust (page 191)

For filling:
2 egg yolks
⅓ cup sugar
2 tablespoons cornstarch

1 cup milk
¼ cup Key lime juice

For topping:
2 ripe kiwis
¼ pound strawberries or cherries

1 carambola (star fruit)
2 sprigs fresh mint leaves

For glaze:
6 tablespoons apricot jam
2 tablespoons water

1 teaspoon lemon juice

To prepare the filling: Beat the egg yolks with a rotary or electric beater and slowly add the sugar. Continue beating until the mixture is nearly white and begins to form a ribbon. (Lift the beaters and form a "W." If this remains on the surface, the ribbon stage has been reached.) Beat in the cornstarch and then the milk. Add the Key lime juice and pour into a saucepan. Bring to a boil over moderate heat, stirring constantly. The sauce will become lumpy as it comes to a boil, and then smooth as you stir. Beat the boiling mixture for 2 to 3 minutes to cook the cornstarch. Remove from the heat and stir for a few minutes until it starts to cool.

To assemble: Spoon the filling into the pie shell. It will be starting to get firm. Peel the kiwis and cut into ¼-inch slices. Wash, hull, and dry the strawberries. Slice in half lengthwise. Wash and dry the carambola and mint leaves. Slice the carambola into little stars. Start along the rim of the pie and make one circle of strawberries, sliced sides down. Make a circle of kiwi slices next to the strawberries. Place several carambola stars in the center, surrounded by mint leaves.

To prepare the glaze: Heat and stir the jam, water, and lemon juice in a heavy-bottomed pan until the jam is melted. While the glaze is very hot, brush it on the fruit, starting from the center and working outward. Refrigerate until ready to serve.

8 to 10 servings.

Key Lime Cake

This recipe is inspired by the many Key lime cakes I have tasted in the Keys. It produces a tangy cake rich in Key lime flavor.

½ cup unsalted butter (1 stick)
1 cup sugar
2 eggs
1¾ cup all-purpose flour
2 teaspoons baking powder
½ teaspoon salt
⅔ cup heavy cream

1 Key lime, with grated rind and juiced to make 1 tablespoon Key lime juice
½ cup Key lime juice
1 cup confectioners' sugar
6-cup Bundt pan or 8-inch square cake pan, 2 inches deep

Grease Bundt pan. Preheat oven to 350 degrees. Cream the butter until smooth. Gradually add the sugar, beating until light and fluffy. Add the eggs, one at a time, and continue to beat. Sift the dry ingredients together. Alternately add the flour and cream into the egg mixture, starting and ending with the flour. Mix in the Key lime rind and 1 tablespoon juice. Spoon the batter into the prepared pan and bake for 20 minutes. Cover the top loosely with a piece of foil to prevent burning and continue to bake for another 20 minutes. The cake is done when a knife or cake tester inserted in the center comes out clean, and the cake starts to pull away from the side. Remove from the oven and let stand 10 minutes. Turn out onto a cake rack to cool.

Meanwhile, prepare the glaze by mixing the ½ cup Key lime juice and the confectioners' sugar together until smooth. While the cake is still warm, slowly spoon the glaze over the top of the cake so that all of the liquid is absorbed. If you place a plate under the cake rack to catch any glaze that runs off, the drippings can be reapplied until all of the liquid has been absorbed. Just before serving, sprinkle with additional confectioners' sugar.

8 servings.

Snook's Key Lime Cheesecake

This is one of pastry chef Karen Punturo's favorite recipes at the Bayside Club, which she and her sister, Pat Mathias, run. It's a large, rich, old-fashioned cheesecake with a tangy Key lime flavor. It is best when eaten two days after baking.

3 cups graham cracker crumbs
1 tablespoon ground ginger
½ cup unsalted butter (1 stick), melted
24 ounces cream cheese, at room temperature
2 cups sugar
1 teaspoon vanilla

8 eggs
4 egg yolks
2 or 3 Key limes or lemons, with grated rind and juiced to make ¾ cup juice
9-inch springform pan

Preheat oven to 300 degrees. Mix the graham crackers and ginger together. Stir the butter into the crumbs. When thoroughly blended, press the crumbs on the bottom and up the side of the springform pan.

In the bowl of an electric mixer, beat the cream cheese, sugar, and vanilla on high speed until fluffy. Reduce the mixer speed and add the eggs and yolks one at a time. Mix in the grated rind and lime juice. Pour the batter into the prepared springform pan. Bake for 1½ hours. Place a piece of foil loosely over the top about halfway through the baking to keep the top from browning. Turn off the oven and leave the cake in it for another hour. Remove and refrigerate until ready to serve. (This cake must be completely cooled before slicing.)

10 to 12 servings.

Key Lime Soufflé

With cushioned rattan chairs, ceiling fans, and the water gently lapping the moonlit beach a few yards away, Little Palm Island at mile marker 28.5 is a dreamy hideaway. Michel Reymond, chef, creates an atmosphere of leisurely tropical elegance and serves a mixture of nouvelle cuisine and local products.

This is a light soufflé, made without egg yolks. It will deflate quickly, so be sure to be ready to serve it immediately.

◆

Sauce

*3 Key limes, grated rind and juiced to make
   ¼ cup juice
⅓ cup sugar
3 tablespoons unsalted butter*

*3 whole eggs
splash of tequila
3 tablespoons cream*

Grate 3 Key limes and squeeze ¼ cup of juice into a stainless steel pot. Add the sugar, butter, and whole eggs. Gently heat to dissolve the sugar. Bring to a boil whisking constantly. Remove from the heat and immediately pour into a bowl and continue to whisk until cool. Add the tequila. Half whip the cream until it just holds its shape and fold into the sauce. Set aside.

◆

Souffle

*butter and sugar to prepare ramekins or
   soufflé dish
5 Key limes, grated rind and juiced to make
   1 cup juice
1 ripe medium banana, thickly sliced
¾ cup sugar*

*2 teaspoons arrowroot
1 tablespoon water
16 egg whites
confectioners' sugar
10 4-ounce ramekins or one 1½-quart soufflé
   dish*

Preheat oven to 375 degrees. Brush a little melted butter on the insides of ramekins or soufflé dish and sprinkle with sugar, shaking out any excess. Grate 5 Key limes and squeeze them to make 1 cup of juice.

Place the grated rind and lime juice in the container of a blender with the banana and process for 1 minute. Pour into a stainless steel saucepan and add the sugar. Heat until the sugar is dissolved, then bring to the boiling point but do not let boil. Mix the arrowroot with the water to make a paste. Add to the mixture. Stir over medium heat until the liquid thickens and is the consistency of very thick cream; do not boil. Set aside in a warm spot.

Whip the egg whites until stiff peaks form. Mix about one-third of the whites into the Key lime mixture, then fold in the remaining whites. Fill the prepared ramekins three-quarters full. Run a toothpick around the edge to help the soufflé rise while cooking. Place on a baking tray in the oven. Bake 15 minutes if using ramekins, 25 minutes if using a soufflé dish. The soufflé should be slightly brown on top and still a little soft in the center. Remove from the oven and sprinkle the top of each soufflé with confectioners' sugar. Place a soufflé in front of each guest and gently open a small hole in the middle with two spoons. Pour a little of the sauce into the hole. Repeat this process with the remaining soufflés.

10 servings.

Key Lime Baked Alaska

André Mueller of Marker 88 took this old standby and, using Keys ingredients, turned it into a local attraction. Before frosting, the mold may be kept for about 30 days in the freezer. After frosting, it will keep 2 days in the freezer.

4 eggs, separated
1 14-ounce can sweetened condensed milk
½ cup Key lime juice
1 quart good quality vanilla ice cream

½ teaspoon cream of tartar
½ cup sugar
⅓ cup toasted almonds or grated chocolate
9 × 5-inch loaf pan

Slightly beat the egg yolks, add condensed milk, and blend. Add Key lime juice and beat well.

Cut the ice cream into 1-inch-thick slices. Place a layer of ice cream in the bottom of a loaf pan and cover with the Key lime mixture. Top with a second layer of ice cream and freeze overnight. Place a baking sheet or ovenproof serving platter in the freezer for about 30 minutes. Unmold the ice cream mixture onto the cold baking sheet. Return to the freezer for at least 1 hour.

Preheat oven to 450 degrees. Beat the egg whites with the cream of tartar until stiff; add the sugar by tablespoons, beating until very stiff. Frost the ice cream with a layer of meringue at least ½ inch thick. Return it to the freezer for 15 minutes. Remove from freezer and immediately place in the oven for 5 minutes or until just golden brown. Top with almonds or chocolate. Serve immediately.

6 to 8 servings.

Key Lime Squares

Bill Gaiser from the Carriage Trade Garden has been making these squares for thirty years. He calls them little yellow brownies.

3 ounces blanched almonds
1 cup unsalted butter (2 sticks)
2¼ cups all-purpose flour
1 tablespoon confectioners' sugar
5 eggs

2 cups sugar
¾ cup Key lime juice
¼ cup confectioners' sugar
8 × 12-inch baking dish

Preheat oven to 350 degrees. Grease baking dish.

Chop the almonds in the container of a food processor and add the butter, flour, and confectioners' sugar. Blend to a dough consistency. Pat into the baking dish and bake for 15 minutes. Meanwhile, gently mix the eggs, sugar, and Key lime juice together, being careful not to let the mixture foam. Remove the baking dish from the oven and reduce temperature to 325 degrees. Pour the lime juice mixture over the partially baked crust and return to the oven. Bake until set, about 20 to 30 minutes. Check that the topping is firm. If it isn't, turn off the oven and leave the pan in the warm oven until the topping firms. Cool. Cut into squares. Sprinkle with confectioners' sugar just before serving.

Makes about 20 squares.

Key Lime Coconut Cookies

Grated unsweetened coconut is available in the frozen food section of many supermarkets. It gives a crunchy texture and coconut flavor to cookies without being too sweet. If you can't find this type of coconut, then use sweetened coconut flakes, but reduce the sugar in the recipe to 1 tablespoon.

1 cup sweetened condensed milk
4 tablespoons Key lime juice
4 tablespoons all-purpose flour

2 cups unsweetened coconut flakes
4 tablespoons sugar

Preheat oven to 350 degrees. Grease 2 baking sheets.

Combine the condensed milk, Key lime juice, and flour in a medium bowl. Stir in the grated coconut and then the sugar. If using sweetened coconut, taste the mixture before adding the sugar. Add the sugar only if you think it is necessary. The cookie should have a tangy flavor from the Key lime juice. Drop teaspoons of the mixture onto the baking sheet, leaving 2 inches between each cookie; they will spread while baking. Bake for 25 minutes until they just start to turn golden. Remove from the pan to a rack to cool. Store in an airtight container.

Makes 30 cookies.

Key Lime Chocolate Chip Ice Cream

Chocolate and Key lime juice complement each other. This ice cream is based on a custard sauce that needs to be prepared and cooled. The secret to a good custard is to cook the sauce patiently and slowly so that it thickens without curdling. It can be made ahead and refrigerated for 3 to 4 days. Homemade ice cream is made without preservatives and emulsifiers and is best eaten on the same day. If kept in the freezer for a while, it will need to be softened before serving. Remove from the freezer and let thaw slightly.

2 cups milk
⅓ cup sugar
1 teaspoon vanilla extract
4 egg yolks

6 tablespoons Key lime juice
1 cup heavy cream
¾ cup chocolate chips

Place the milk, sugar, and vanilla in a saucepan and warm until the sugar completely dissolves. Whisk the egg yolks in a bowl and very slowly pour in about ½ cup of the milk, whisking constantly. Pour the mixture into the milk in the saucepan and cook over low heat, stirring constantly, for about 15 minutes until the custard sauce thickens and coats the back of a spoon. (This means that when you draw your finger over the back of the spoon, a clear line remains.) Strain the sauce into a bowl and let cool. Mix in the Key lime juice and refrigerate. When the mixture is cold, whip the cream until it just holds its shape and fold into the custard. Place in the container of an ice-cream freezer and process until thick. Otherwise, pour the mixture into a metal bowl and place in the freezer. When it begins to set, remove and beat, then return to the freezer. Repeat this process two more times until the ice cream is thick.

Coarsely chop the chocolate bits. When the cream is thick, fold in the chocolate and pour into a plastic container or ice-cream mold. Freeze until ready to use.

8 to 10 servings.

Key Lime Sorbet

Key limes, with their fragrance and fresh flavor, make a wonderful sorbet. When experimenting with this sorbet, I added one tablespoon of Chambord to one batch and a tablespoon of curaçao to another. They both were a great success. Use the basic recipe below, but add one of the liqueurs to the Key lime juice prior to mixing it with the sugar syrup.

1⅔ cups granulated sugar	1 cup Key lime juice
1½ cups water	2 egg whites

Combine the sugar and water in a heavy-bottomed saucepan over medium heat. Stir occasionally until the sugar is dissolved. Bring the syrup to a boil, removing the saucepan from the heat as soon as a full boil is reached. Set aside to cool. You should have about 2 cups sugar syrup.

Stir the Key lime juice into the sugar syrup. Refrigerate the syrup until cold, and then pour it into the container of an ice-cream freezer and follow instructions for freezing. Otherwise, pour the mixture into a metal bowl and place in the freezer; remove and whip every few hours. When the mixture is partly frozen, beat the egg whites to a stiff peak and fold into the mixture. Continue to freeze. The sorbet is best made one day before serving. If kept longer, remove it from the freezer about 12 hours before you intend to serve it, let it soften and reblend it in the food processor before refreezing it.

8 servings.

Key Lime Fudge Sauce

Mixing tart Key lime juice into rich, dark chocolate makes a delicious fudge sauce.

1⅔ cups sugar
1 5-ounce can evaporated milk
3 ounces semisweet chocolate

2 tablespoons butter
2 tablespoons Key lime juice

Dissolve the sugar in the milk over medium heat. Stir in the chocolate and butter and cook until the sauce is smooth. Remove from heat and stir in the Key lime juice. Cool and refrigerate in a jar until needed.

The sauce can be rewarmed in a microwave or over hot water and used to spoon over ice cream, sorbet, or plain cake; or as a dip for fruit.

Makes about 1¼ cups sauce.

Other Desserts

Rum Mango Ice Cream 221

Passion Fruit Sorbet 222

Mango Sorbet 223

Mangoes Morada 224

Hawk's Cay Fruit Kebabs with Coconut Dip 225

Passion Fruit Bread 226

Snook's Bayside Club Strawberry Bread 227

Avocado Bread 228

Mango Coconut Bread 229

Margaret Stevens's Bimini Bread 230

Passion Fruit Pie—Cheeca Lodge

Susan Waterman, sous chef at Cheeca Lodge, gave me this recipe. It has become my favorite dessert. Unless you're an incurable chocoholic, I think it will become yours, too.

Each passion fruit gives about 2 tablespoons of juice. The best way to juice them is to cut off the top and scoop out the pulp. Place in a blender or food processor to break the seed sacs and then push through a strainer. You can do this in one step if you have a food mill. Passion fruit freezes beautifully. Simply place the fruit in a plastic bag in the freezer. They defrost as if they had just been picked. Frozen passion fruit pulp is available in many specialty stores or in Hispanic food markets, where it is called *parcha,* and is a good substitute in this recipe.

4 eggs
1 cup sugar
¾ cup passion fruit puree or pulp (about 12 fruits)
¼ cup Key lime juice (or lime juice)

½ cup cold unsalted butter (1 stick)
1 envelope unflavored gelatin
¼ cup water
Graham Cracker Pie Crust (page 192)

Mix the eggs, sugar, passion fruit puree, and lime juice together in the top of a double boiler. Place over hot water and cook until it begins to thicken. Cut the butter into 8 pieces and gradually add to the sauce as it thickens, stirring constantly. Soften the gelatin in water; stir into the hot sauce to dissolve. Let cool and pour into the prepared graham cracker crust. Refrigerate until firm, at least 2 hours. Top the pie with whipped cream, meringue, or chocolate curls and serve at room temperature to get the full flavor of the fruit.

8 to 10 servings.

Cuban Banana–Rum Custard Tart

Doug Shook wanted a Caribbean dessert for Louie's Backyard in Key West. What could be more tropical than rum and bananas? He used Cuban bananas (see Glossary). They are juicier and sweeter than regular or Cavendish bananas, but regular bananas can be substituted.

◆

Cashew Pastry

½ cup butter (1 stick), softened
2 tablespoons sugar
1 egg, lightly beaten
½ teaspoon vanilla extract

1½ cups all-purpose flour
5 ounces unsalted cashews, finely chopped
  (about 1 cup)

Beat the butter and sugar in an electric mixer or by hand until fluffy. Add the egg and vanilla and continue beating. Mix in the flour and the cashews. The mixture will be soft and cannot be rolled out. Press the dough into the pie plate with your fingertips, keeping it as evenly distributed as possible. Chill for 30 minutes.

Preheat oven to 350 degrees. Place foil in the shell and fill it with dried beans or rice. Bake for 15 minutes; remove the foil and beans and bake 5 more minutes. Set aside to cool.

Makes one 8-inch pie crust.

◆

Custard

2 eggs
⅓ cup sugar
2 tablespoons all-purpose flour
¾ cup heavy cream
4 tablespoons dark rum

4 Cuban bananas, peeled and sliced
½ cup apricot preserves
1 orange, juiced
8-inch pie plate

Beat the eggs and sugar until light and frothy. Mix in the flour and beat until smooth. Add the cream and rum. Pour into the partially baked crust and bake in a preheated oven at 350 degrees for about 20 minutes or until the custard is set. Remove and cool. Arrange the bananas on the top, starting from the outside and working toward the center.

Warm the preserves and orange juice, stirring until the preserves have melted. Strain and brush the tart with the hot glaze to protect the bananas from turning brown and to add a sheen to the tart.

12 servings.

Coconut Custard Pie—Lovin' Dough Restaurant

This extra-easy dessert seems to have been in every grandmother's recipe box. The ingredients are simply beaten together and poured into a pie plate. The baked pie has the crust and custard where they belong. There are many versions, most calling for Bisquick, which makes me think the recipe originated with General Mills. All-purpose flour with 1 teaspoon baking powder can be substituted. The Lovin' Dough Restaurant makes these pies for sale in their bakery and restaurant. Here is their version.

2 cups milk
4 eggs
½ cup butter (1 stick), cut into small pieces
1 teaspoon vanilla

¾ cup sugar
½ cup biscuit mix (such as Bisquick)
1 cup sweetened coconut flakes

Preheat oven to 350 degrees. Grease a 9-inch pie plate.

Place the ingredients, except the coconut, in the container of a blender and process for 3 minutes. Pour the mixture into the pie plate and let sit for 5 minutes. Sprinkle the coconut on top and bake for 60 minutes or until the coconut is golden brown and the custard set. If the coconut starts to become too brown before the custard is done, place a piece of foil loosely over the top until the pie is cooked. Chill pie. Remove from refrigerator 30 minutes before serving so that pie is at room temperature.

8 servings.

Strawberry Pie

Mary and Stan's has been an institution in Key Largo since 1953. Their son, Don, and his wife, Lucille, now run the restaurant with the same style of cooking. The Chrzan's were originally from Poland, and Don still makes and smokes his own Polish sausages. It's a two-day process. He prepares them one day and then smokes them over hickory and buttonwood the next. If you're in the area, try their kielbasa sandwiches, served on rye bread with potato salad on the side.

Strawberries grow abundantly near Homestead, just a few miles from Key Largo, and strawberry pie often appears on the menu at Mary and Stan's. This recipe is my variation, inspired by Lucille's love of fresh strawberries. The berries are not cooked and their freshness is sealed in by the sauce.

1 9-inch baked pie shell	*1 cup water*
3 pounds ripe strawberries	*½ cup whipping cream*
1 cup sugar	*1 tablespoon sugar*
4 tablespoons cornstarch	

Prepare a pie shell, using a frozen pre-made shell or Sweet Pastry Crust (see page 191). Wash and hull strawberries. Slice and fill the baked pie shell with the best ones, reserving 2 cups for the sauce. Combine the sugar and cornstarch in a medium saucepan. Add the water and cook until the liquid thickens. Add the 2 cups of reserved strawberries and continue to cook about 5 minutes until a thick red sauce is formed. Spoon the sauce over the strawberry-filled pie and place in the refrigerator to set. Just before serving, whip the cream until soft peaks form. Add the sugar and continue whipping until stiff. Serve with the pie.

8 servings.

Frances Wolfson's Lime Chiffon Pie

Persian limes, better known simply as limes, are a major Florida crop and are sold in abundance year-round. To give her pie a more intense lime flavor Frances Wolfson used the grated rind as well as the juice for her Lime Chiffon Pie. Typical of Keys cooking, this chiffon pie is made with sweetened condensed milk. It's easy to make and has a fresh citrus flavor.

1 15½-ounce can sweetened condensed milk
3 eggs, separated
4 to 6 fresh limes, grated rind and juiced to
*   make ½ cup fresh lime juice*

1 tablespoon gelatin
¼ cup cold water
9- to 10-inch Graham Cracker Pie Crust
*   (page 192)*

In a medium-size bowl whip the condensed milk and egg yolks until thoroughly combined. Add the grated rind and lime juice. Soften the gelatin in the water in a metal measuring cup and place over low heat in a water-filled skillet until gelatin has dissolved. Stir the gelatin into the filling and spoon into the graham cracker crust. Refrigerate until set, at least 2 hours. This may be made a day ahead.

8 to 10 servings.

Piña Colada Cheesecake

A cool piña colada, a beach chair, and the turquoise sea are the ingredients for a perfect Keys holiday. Rum distilled from sugar cane has been part of Keys culture since early rum-running days. Mixed with tropical fruits such as coconut and pineapple, rum makes a delicious drink. Mary Ballard, from Ganim's restaurant, took the ingredients for the popular piña colada and created a light and tasty cheesecake.

◆

Coconut Crust

2¼ cups bread crumbs or vanilla wafer
   crumbs*
1½ cups flaked sweetened coconut

½ cup butter or margarine, melted
9- or 10-inch springform pan

Preheat oven to 350 degrees. Combine the ingredients and mix well. Line the bottom and side of a springform pan with the crumbs, pressing together with a spoon. Bake for 10 minutes and set aside to cool.

Makes enough to line a 9- or 10-inch springform pan.

◆

Piña Colada Filling

2 envelopes gelatin
¾ cup sugar
1 6-ounce can pineapple juice
3 eggs, separated
24 ounces cream cheese

½ cup cream of coconut
⅓ cup rum
1 20-ounce can crushed pineapple
2 tablespoons sugar
1 tablespoon cornstarch

Mix the gelatin and ½ cup sugar in a saucepan. Add the pineapple juice and place over very low heat to dissolve sugar and gelatin. Do not boil. Beat the egg yolks in a large bowl, gradually adding the gelatin mixture. Let cool. In a second bowl beat the cream cheese until fluffy and

*Making the crust with bread crumbs gives a crust with just a hint of sweetness once the coconut is mixed in. Use whichever ingredient suits your palate.

add gelatin mixture, cream of coconut, and rum. Blend well. Refrigerate until the mixture starts to gel. Beat the egg whites until they form soft peaks. Add the remaining ¼ cup sugar gradually, continuing to beat until the egg whites form stiff peaks. Fold the whites into gelatin mixture. Spoon the filling into the prepared springform pan and refrigerate until set.

Combine the crushed pineapple, 2 tablespoons sugar, and cornstarch in a saucepan. Cook over low heat, stirring constantly, until the sauce comes to a boil, thickens, and becomes clear. Cool and spoon over the top of the cheesecake. The cake will keep 2 days in the refrigerator. When ready to serve, run a knife around the edge of the pan and remove the side. Place the cheesecake on serving platter and serve.

12 to 15 servings.

Jamaican Sauce for Pound Cake

Diane Pansire, owner-chef of Rich's Cafe at the Eden House in Key West, served this cake to the movie moguls when they were redecorating the hotel to its sixties style for filming. The curry and rum give this sauce its intriguing flavor, and it's a delicious topping for a pound cake.

¾ teaspoon curry powder	*¼ cup sour cream*
½ cup light rum	*4 bananas, peeled and sliced ¼ inch thick*
¾ cup heavy cream	*1 teaspoon sugar*
2 ounces cream cheese	*8 slices of pound cake*

Heat the curry powder in a saucepan a few seconds and then add the rum. When the rum is hot, flame it. (If using a gas stove, tip the pan and the flames will light the rum. For an electric burner, throw a lighted match in the hot rum to light it. Be sure to remove the match later.) Add the cream, cream cheese, and sour cream, stirring until the mixture bubbles and reduces slightly. Add the bananas to the sauce with the sugar. Taste and add more sugar if necessary. Place two slices of pound cake each on four individual plates and spoon the sauce on top.

4 servings.

Duval Café con Leche Cake

The Café upstairs at Louie's Backyard in Key West is a casual restaurant. They serve Spanish-Caribbean cuisine and their Café con Leche Cake has become well known. This coffee-flavored cake is served in a cappuccino cup, and you have to look twice to see if it is cake or coffee.

The cake and syrup can be made ahead and warmed just before serving.

◆

Espresso Cakes

¾ cup all-purpose flour
¼ cup finely ground espresso coffee beans
1 teaspoon instant espresso powder
½ teaspoon baking powder
¼ teaspoon salt
½ cup ground almonds

4 large eggs, separated
¾ cup sugar
1 teaspoon vanilla extract
4 tablespoons unsalted butter (½ stick), melted
   and cooled
12-cup muffin pan

Preheat oven to 350 degrees. Butter a 12-cup muffin pan and set aside.

Sift the flour, espresso ground beans and powder, baking powder, and salt together. Stir in the ground almonds. Whip the egg yolks and 6 tablespoons of the sugar together until pale and thick. Mix in the vanilla. Add the flour mixture all at once to the egg yolks and fold in. Add the butter all at once and continue to fold until all of the ingredients are incorporated. Beat the egg whites until frothy, then slowly add the remaining sugar, beating until stiff. Fold the beaten egg whites into the batter. Fill the muffin cups to the top. Bake 20 to 25 minutes until the cakes spring back when touched in the center. Remove the cakes from the pan and cool on a wire rack.

◆

Coffee Syrup

⅔ cup sugar

⅔ cup water

½ cup coffee-flavored liqueur

Combine the sugar and water in a small saucepan and bring to a boil, stirring until the sugar is dissolved. Cool. Add the coffee liqueur.

Makes about 1½ cups syrup.

◆

Cooking and Serving

2¼ cups heavy cream, whipped but still
   pourable

ground cinnamon

grated chocolate

12 6-ounce cappuccino cups

When ready to serve, preheat oven to 375 degrees. Place an espresso cake into each of 12 large cappuccino cups. Pour 2 tablespoons Coffee Syrup over each cake. Place the cups on a baking sheet and heat for 10 minutes. Remove the cups from the oven, cover each cake with whipped cream, and dust the top with cinnamon and grated chocolate. Place on a saucer and serve, warning guests that the cups are hot.

12 servings.

Reta's Famous Flan

Reta Sawyer is a southern belle from Atlanta who married into an old Conch family and is fascinated with Spanish and Cuban foods. Just after World War II she and her husband often traveled to Havana, where she learned about Cuban food. She has incorporated her good southern cooking background with some hints from the native Conchs and her love of Hispanic cooking into her own style of cooking.

Reta's flan is a popular addition to many Keys parties. It can be made in a food processor or blender, but unless you have an oversized machine, you will need to mix the ingredients in two stages. This makes a very large flan, but the ingredients can easily be halved to serve a smaller number of guests.

2 cups sugar	*2 4½-ounce cans sweetened condensed milk*
½ cup water	*9 ounces water (2 condensed milk canfuls)*
1 pound cream cheese	*2 teaspoons vanilla extract*
12 eggs	*9-inch springform pan*

Place sugar and ½ cup water in a heavy-bottomed saucepan and cook over low heat until the sugar is dissolved. The water should not boil before the sugar is dissolved and the liquid is absolutely clear. Raise the heat and boil the sugar solution until it becomes golden in color. Pour the syrup into a 9-inch springform pan, tipping the pan to make sure the bottom and side are covered with caramel. Set aside to harden.

Preheat oven to 325 degrees. Place the remaining ingredients in the container of a blender or food processor and mix until smooth. Depending upon the size of your machine, you may have to do this in batches. Pour the mixture into the prepared pan and place in a roasting pan. Put the pan on the rack in your preheated oven and pour boiling water into the roasting pan, about three-quarters up the side of the springform pan. Bake for 1 hour. The flan should be nearly firm. If it appears loose, bake for another 15 to 20 minutes. Cool on a cake rack. The custard will set as it cools. It can be refrigerated overnight and served the next day. To turn out, run a spatula around the edge of the pan and place a serving plate over the top. Turn upside down and give it one firm shake. The flan will easily come out of the mold with the caramelized sugar, which becomes the sauce.

20 servings.

Sally's Mango Pudding

The warm breezes and Keys ambiance brought Sally Thomas to Key West in 1981. She was fascinated by the tropical fruits, especially the mango tree outside her kitchen window. One year a bumper crop sent her scurrying for new recipes. She had already made enough chutney for every friend she had. Mango Pudding was one result of her search. It can be served as a pudding or poured into a baked pie shell and served as a mango pie.

1 18-ounce can mangoes, drained
1 14½-ounce can sweetened condensed milk
⅓ cup Key lime juice or ordinary lime juice

2 medium-size ripe mangoes, peeled and cut
into 1-inch pieces (see Glossary)
2 egg whites

Puree the canned mangoes with the milk and lime juice in the container of a food processor or blender. Add the cut-up ripe mangoes to the mixture and puree until smooth and thick. Remove the mixture to a large bowl. Beat the egg whites until stiff peaks form and fold into the mango mixture. Spoon into individual ramekins or pudding dishes, or a large bowl or soufflé dish. Chill for at least 2 hours before serving.

8 to 10 servings.

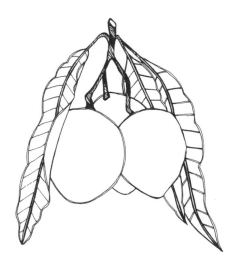

Bobbie Sawyer's Natilla

"This dessert takes ten minutes to make and ten minutes to eat," explained Bobbie Sawyer. Bobbie's great grandparents came from Spain to Cuba and then made their way to Key West in the late 1800's. She married into the Sawyers, a well-known Conch family. This recipe has been part of Bobbie's family for years. She can remember her mother and grandmother making it. One tradition that remains vivid in her memory is her mother putting a piece of lime peel in the pudding to give it extra flavor; the child who found it got a quarter, which was big money in those days. Natilla is a light, smooth, and delicious dessert.

1 14-ounce can sweetened condensed milk
14 ounces water (1 condensed milk canful)
1 13-ounce can evaporated milk
3 egg yolks
3 rounded tablespoons cornstarch

3 tablespoons water
2½ teaspoons vanilla extract
2 tablespoons unsalted butter
ground cinnamon

Combine the condensed milk, water, evaporated milk, and egg yolks in a saucepan. In a cup mix the cornstarch with 3 tablespoons water to form a smooth paste and add to the mixture. Bring to a boil, stirring constantly with a whisk, and cook until the mixture begins to thicken and is difficult to stir. Remove from the heat and stir in the vanilla and butter. Pour into small cups, ramekins, or a soufflé dish. Sprinkle with cinnamon and refrigerate until ready to serve.

14 servings.

Pudin de Pan, Bread Pudding La Lechonera

Every culture has its own form of bread pudding. It is a nursery dish in England and appears on most Cuban menus. It is usually made with milk, but like many Keys dishes that are throwbacks to the days when the lack of refrigeration made fresh milk scarce, La Lechonera's pudding is made with evaporated milk. The addition of guava paste is another special touch to their recipe. Guava has an intense flavor and a meaty texture. It also has a lot of pectin and is made into a paste with very concentrated flavor. The paste can be found in cans or long thin narrow boxes in most supermarkets. Substitute guava jelly or, if this is unavailable, try quince or red currant jelly. If using jelly or jam as a substitute, only use about half the amount of sugar called for in the recipe.

¼ pound Cuban or white bread (about 7 slices)	*1 teaspoon vanilla extract*
1 13-ounce can evaporated milk	*1 cup raisins*
5 eggs	*¾ cup butter (1½ sticks), melted*
¾ cup sugar	*1 pound guava paste, thinly sliced*
	8-inch round pudding or soufflé dish

Preheat oven to 350 degrees. Soak the bread in a bowl of water. Combine the milk, eggs, half of the sugar, and vanilla in medium-sized bowl. Taste for sweetness, adding more sugar as needed. Rinse raisins and drain. Pour half of the melted butter into pudding or soufflé dish and mix the rest into the milk with the raisins. Squeeze the water from the bread and layer half of it in the bottom of the pudding dish. Layer half of the guava paste on top of the bread. Pour some of the milk mixture into the pan and layer the remaining bread and guava paste. Pour in the rest of the milk mixture. Bake for about 40 minutes or until the bread is firm.

8 to 10 servings.

Queen of All Puddings

"Our family always fixes this bread pudding during Thanksgiving and Christmas and on special occasions . . . it's so colorful and decorative and it's the best in Key West," says Bobbie Sawyer about this well-known Key West recipe. In fact, it's an extra-rich bread pudding with red and green glacé cherries and pecans. This recipe will easily feed 12, but can be cut in half. You can substitute French or Italian bread for Cuban bread.

6 eggs
½ 14-ounce can sweetened condensed milk
½ 5-ounce can evaporated milk
1 tablespoon vanilla extract
1 pound sugar
1 quart milk
1 teaspoon ground nutmeg
2 teaspoons ground cinnamon
8 cups Cuban bread chunks (about ¾ loaf)

8 ounces guava paste, cut into small squares
  (half of a 1-pound box)
1 cup pecans, chopped
½ cup red glacé cherries
½ cup green glacé cherries
ground nutmeg and ground cinnamon for
  decoration
1 2½-quart pudding dish or baking pan, or 1
  9 × 13-inch baking dish

Preheat oven to 350 degrees. Combine all of the ingredients except the bread, guava paste, pecans, and cherries. Add the bread and make sure it is thoroughly soaked into the mixture. Mix thoroughly. If the mixture appears too thick, add a little water. Butter the baking dish and pour in the mixture. Add the guava paste, pushing some to the bottom of the pan and leaving some on the top. Add the two types of cherries on top, along with the pecans. Sprinkle the top with nutmeg and cinnamon. Cover the pan with foil and bake for 1 hour. Uncover and bake for another 30 minutes or until golden brown on top.

12 servings.

Rum Mango Ice Cream

From May through September you can see sweet mangoes hanging from their trees all throughout South Dade and the Keys. This is a typical Keys recipe because it uses sweetened condensed milk. I added some rum to one of my batches and found that it was delicious.

2 cups pureed ripe mangoes (see Glossary)
1 14-ounce can sweetened condensed milk
1 cup heavy cream

¼ cup brown sugar
6 tablespoons dark rum
1 tablespoon lime juice

Combine the ingredients in a medium-size bowl and stir to blend. Pour into the container of an ice-cream freezer and freeze according to instructions. Otherwise, pour the mixture into a metal bowl and place in the freezer. After about 2 hours, beat the mixture and then replace in the freezer. Do this two more times or until the mixture is thick. Place in a plastic container or ice cream mold, cover, and leave in the freezer until ready to use.

8 servings.

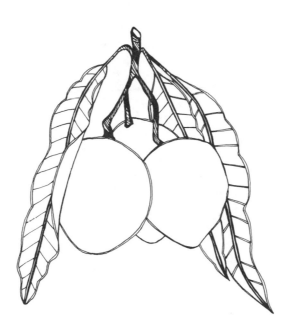

Passion Fruit Sorbet

Passion fruit is one of the most intensely flavored of the tropical fruits. Wrinkling is a natural ripening characteristic. Frozen passion fruit pulp can be found in some supermarkets or Latin markets.

2½ cups sugar
2 cups water

1 cup strained passion fruit puree from about 2½ pounds fruit (see Glossary)
1 cup still mineral water

Place the sugar and water in a saucepan over low heat until the sugar is dissolved. Raise the heat and bring the liquid to a full boil; remove from heat. Cool. Add the puree to the sugar syrup along with the mineral water. Pour into the container of an ice-cream freezer and freeze according to instructions. Otherwise, pour the mixture into a metal bowl and place in the freezer. Take out and whip every few hours as it begins to freeze. Sorbet is best made 1 day before serving. If kept longer, take the sorbet out of the freezer about 12 hours before you intend using it, let it soften, reblend it with a food processor, and refreeze.

8 to 10 servings.

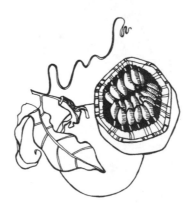

Mango Sorbet

Most tropical fruits can be made into refreshing sorbets. I like to make several different kinds and serve a scoop of each on a dish along with an array of fresh fruit to make a light and colorful dessert for a party.

Try this recipe with soursop, carambola, lychees, or papaya. The basic recipe remains the same; simply substitute the different fruit pulps for the mango.

2½ cups sugar
2 cups water

3 cups pulp from about 4 mangoes (see
Glossary)
1 lime, juiced

Place the sugar and water in a saucepan over low heat until the sugar is dissolved. Raise the heat and bring the liquid to a full boil; remove from heat. Cool. Puree the mangoes with the sugar syrup and add the lime juice. Taste and add more lime juice if the mixture seems too sweet. Pour into the container of an ice-cream freezer and freeze according to instructions. Otherwise, pour the mixture into a metal bowl and place in the freezer. Take out and whip every few hours as it begins to freeze. Sorbet is best made 1 day before serving. If kept longer, take the sorbet out of the freezer about 12 hours before you intend to use it, let it soften, reblend it with a food processor, and refreeze.

8 servings.

Mangoes Morada

Mango maniacs will love this easy tropical dessert. It's named for Islamorada, the home of Marker 88. Mangoes were introduced to South Florida in 1860 and are used extensively in Keys cooking. If desired, substitute your favorite chocolate sauce for mine, or try the Key Lime Fudge Sauce on page 203.

4 large scoops, best vanilla ice cream
2 large, ripe mangoes, peeled and cubed (see Glossary)
½ cup Chocolate Sauce (recipe follows)

½ cup slivered almonds, toasted
½ teaspoon cinnamon
¼ cup Grand Marnier
1 cup heavy cream, whipped

Place a large scoop of ice cream in each of 4 individual dishes. Top each scoop with mango cubes. Warm the chocolate sauce and toss the toasted almonds with the cinnamon. Spoon the warm chocolate sauce and the Grand Marnier and almonds on top of the ice cream. Surround with whipped cream.

4 servings.

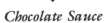

Chocolate Sauce

6 ounces good quality semisweet chocolate
⅔ cup water

½ cup sugar
1 teaspoon vanilla

Break the chocolate into small pieces and place in a heavy-bottomed saucepan with the water and sugar. Cook over low heat until the chocolate is melted and the sugar dissolved; mix well. Bring the sauce to a simmer and cook gently for 10 to 15 minutes or until thickened. Do not let the sauce boil rapidly. Mix in the vanilla. Use immediately or store in a glass jar in the refrigerator and rewarm over water or in a microwave.

Makes about 1 cup sauce.

Hawk's Cay Fruit Kebabs with Coconut Dip

Hawk's Cay is nestled on an island in the heart of the Keys at mile marker 61. This recipe uses an abundance of tropical fruit combined with a coconut and rum dip to make a light and delicious dessert that could also be served as a garnish for a meat course.

Any type of fresh, ripe fruit may be used in this recipe. For a large crowd, Hawk's Cay serves these skewers in a pineapple shell. They cut the pineapple in half lengthwise, leaving the leaves intact. The fruit is removed and the shell halves are placed cut sides up and slightly raised at one end as a centerpiece on the table. The finished fruit kebabs are placed in the shells so that it looks like a cornucopia filled with fruit.

1 fresh pineapple, peeled and cubed
3 bananas, thickly sliced
3 carambola or star fruit, thickly sliced
1 papaya, peeled, seeded, and cubed
6 strawberries
1 cup pineapple juice
½ cup honey

2 tablespoons Cointreau
1 teaspoon chopped fresh mint
1 cup whipping cream
1 tablespoon Coco Lopez, cream of coconut
1 tablespoon dark rum
½ cup coconut flakes

Put the prepared fruits in a bowl just large enough to hold them. Combine the pineapple juice, honey, Cointreau, and chopped mint and pour over the fruit. Marinate for 30 minutes, gently stirring the pieces from time to time to make sure they are evenly coated with the mixture. Meanwhile, whip the cream until soft peaks form. Gradually add the cream of coconut and rum and beat until stiff. Spoon the whipped cream into a serving or dipping bowl. Spread the coconut on a baking sheet and place in a 350-degree oven for 3 to 4 minutes until the flakes start to turn golden. Sprinkle on top of the cream. Skewer the fruits, alternating the colors to make an attractive arrangement. Place on a hot grill for 5 minutes, turning them once and basting with the marinade. Alternatively, the fruit may be placed under a hot broiler for the same amount of time. Be sure to watch the fruit so that it doesn't turn black. Serve the kebabs with the Coconut Dip.

6 servings.

Passion Fruit Bread

Passion fruit's intense flavor combined with the carambola's tartness makes this bread unique.

2¼ cups unbleached, sifted all-purpose flour
¾ cup sugar
2¼ teaspoon baking powder
½ teaspoon salt
¼ teaspoon baking soda

1 cup passion fruit puree or
  pulp (about 12 fruits)
1 egg
2 tablespoons butter or margarine, melted
1 ripe carambola (star fruit), thinly sliced
8½ × 4½-inch loaf pan

Preheat oven to 350 degrees. Grease and flour the loaf pan.

Sift the flour, sugar, baking powder, salt, and baking soda into a mixing bowl. Combine the passion fruit puree, egg, and melted butter in a second mixing bowl. Reserve 8 of the best carambola stars and chop the rest, adding them to the passion fruit mixture. Turn the liquid ingredients into the dry ones, stirring just until the dry ingredients are moist; be careful not to overmix. Spoon into the prepared loaf pan. Place the reserved stars as close together as possible on the top. Bake for 1 hour. Check after 40 minutes and if the top looks a little brown, cover it loosely with a piece of foil. The bread is done when it begins to shrink away from the sides of the pan and a wooden pick inserted into the middle comes out clean. Remove from the oven and let stand 5 minutes. Turn out onto a cake rack to cool completely.

10 servings.

Snook's Bayside Club Strawberry Bread

Drive by the fields around Homestead, Florida, during the season and you can smell the strawberries ripening. Homestead is the mainland city just north of the Keys and these luscious, bright-red berries are used extensively in Keys cooking. Pat, chef and partner at Snook's Bayside Club, says this bread is so good and so easy to make that she finds it hard to pass up a chance to bake some when strawberries are in season.

3 cups all-purpose flour
2 cups sugar
3 teaspoons cinnamon
1 teaspoon baking soda
1 teaspoon salt
1¼ cups vegetable oil

4 eggs
1¼ pounds fresh strawberries, sliced, or
*   unsweetened frozen berries, thawed,*
*   thoroughly drained, and coarsely chopped*
½ cup walnuts, coarsely chopped
2 8½ × 4½-inch loaf pans

Preheat oven to 350 degrees. Grease and flour the two loaf pans.

Mix the flour, sugar, cinnamon, baking soda, and salt in a large mixing bowl. Add the oil, eggs, strawberries, and walnuts. Beat until the dry ingredients are just moist. Pour into the prepared loaf pans and bake for 1 hour. The breads are done when they start to come away from the sides of the pans and an inserted wooden pick comes out clean.

Makes 2 loaves.

Avocado Bread

If you like to explore, get off the main road when driving through the Keys and find some of the little off-the-track restaurants. At the end of Transylvania Avenue on the ocean side in Key Largo, you'll come to a little restaurant with a screened porch overlooking the ocean. It is next door to the Undersea Park. Barry Richman found a perfect name for his little restaurant, the Hideout. It's open for lunch and dinner and is a casual place to stop and enjoy a light meal and the spectacular view. Gerri Richman loves to bake and gave me this bread recipe.

When large buttery avocados come into season in the Keys, everyone starts looking for new ways to use their backyard crops. This is a moist and delicious bread that fills the bill.

¾ cup mashed ripe avocados (about 2)
3 eggs
1 cup vegetable oil
3 teaspoons vanilla
3 cups all-purpose flour
1½ cups sugar

2 teaspoons cinnamon
1 teaspoon salt
1 teaspoon baking soda
½ teaspoon baking powder
¾ cup walnuts, chopped
9 × 5-inch loaf pan

Preheat oven to 350 degrees. Grease the loaf pan and set aside.

Mash the avocados and mix with the eggs, oil, and vanilla. Blend well. Add the flour, sugar, cinnamon, salt, baking soda, and baking powder. Fold in the nuts. Bake for 1½ hours. Cover the top loosely with foil after the first 30 minutes.

Makes 1 loaf.

Mango Coconut Bread

Here is a moist bread with a subtle mango flavor combined with that of coconuts and macadamia nuts.

1 cup sugar
2 eggs
½ cup vegetable oil
1 cup all-purpose flour
1 teaspoon baking soda
1 teaspoon cinnamon
¼ teaspoon salt

1 cup pureed ripe mangoes (see Glossary)
¼ cup shredded coconut
¼ cup macadamia nuts or walnuts
½ teaspoon vanilla
8½ × 4½-inch loaf pan or 18 2-ounce muffin
*   cups*

Preheat oven to 350 degrees. Grease the loaf pan or muffin cups.

Beat the sugar and eggs together; add the oil and continue to beat. Sift the flour with the baking soda, cinnamon, and salt. Gradually add to the egg mixture. Add the remaining ingredients and blend. Fill the loaf pan or muffin pans. Bake the loaf pan one hour, the muffin tins 20 minutes.

Makes 1 loaf or 18 muffins.

Margaret Stevens's Bimini Bread

Margaret Stevens started selling her Key lime jelly outside a Chevron Station near the Holiday Isle resort. She added her Key lime and rum cakes to her repertoire and Holiday Isle offered her a little hut to sell her homemade goods. That was about 22 years ago. Now, with the help of her children, she runs Lovin' Dough, Inc., Restaurant and Bakery, where they still serve homemade food along with jellies and cakes.

A young Bahamian woman who ran a resort in the Exumas came to visit Margaret about 17 years ago and made this bread for her. Margaret has been serving it in her restaurant ever since.

⅓ cup boiling water
¼ cup sweetened coconut
2 cups all-purpose flour
⅓ cup sugar

1 package rapid rising yeast
6 tablespoons butter (¾ stick), melted
1 egg
8½ × 4½-inch loaf pan

Pour the boiling water over the sweetened coconut and let steep for 5 minutes to make coconut milk. In a large bowl, combine 1 cup of the flour with the sugar and yeast. Strain the coconut milk into the melted butter and heat to tepid; it will feel just slightly warm to the touch. This can be done in a microwave. Stir the butter mixture into the flour mixture and add the egg. Beat well. Add the rest of the flour a little at a time until the dough is no longer sticky; you may need a little more flour. Knead the dough until it is elastic, at least 10 minutes. Cover and let rest for 10 minutes. Grease the loaf pan. Deflate the dough with your fist and shape into a loaf. Place in the prepared pan.

Preheat oven to 325 degrees. Cover the pan with a towel and place in a warm spot to rise until double in size. Bake for 40 minutes or until the top of the bread is a light golden brown and a cake tester inserted in the center comes out clean. Remove from the pan and let cool on a cake rack.

8 servings.

Glossary

Annatto Also known as achiote, this is a dried red seed that is ground and used mostly for coloring.

Bijol This is a substitute for saffron. It is yellow and made from ground annatto seed, and often contains some cumin and oregano. Tumeric can be used as a substitute.

Boniato Boniato is a type of tropical sweet potato. Its smooth-textured flesh is only slightly sweet and has a buttery, nutty flavor. Boniatos can be cooked in the same manner as any type of potato; they give an intriguing flavor to soups and stews. Try to buy small boniatos, which are tenderer than the larger ones.

Carambola The carambola, also known as star fruit or star apple, looks something like a short squat banana with fins when it is whole. When it is cut crosswise, the slices look like perfectly shaped yellow stars. They provide a fresh fragrance and a sweet and tart flavor. There are many varieties, some sweeter than others. Since the development of sweet carambolas, the fruit has become very popular and is sold throughout the United States in supermarkets and specialty food stores. Biting into a ripe one is like taking a refreshing drink. They make pretty garnishes, are great in stir-frys, and add sparkle to sauces. Carambolas are in season from August through February.

Chayote This tropical squash looks like a green gnarled pear and has been traced to the Aztec and Mayan cultures. It belongs to the squash and cucumber family and can be used in the same manner as these vegetables. It can be peeled and grated, boiled and stuffed, or sliced and used instead of water chestnuts in stir-frys. It has a slightly citrus tang when you bite into it and is available year-round. Use squash as a substitute.

Chorizo A spicy Cuban sausage usually made from pork and liver. Any type of spicy sausage can be used as a substitute.

Cilantro Cilantro, also known as coriander and Chinese parsley, looks very much like flat parsley. It has a very distinct flavor and is widely used in South and Central American cooking. It is readily available in most supermarkets now.

Clarified Butter Clarified butter is made by melting butter and discarding the milk solids. To do this, heat 2 tablespoons butter until it foams. Pour into a bowl to cool. The sediment that falls to the bottom should be scraped away from the cooled fat. The clarified butter will keep for months in the refrigerator or freezer. It will also reach a high temperature without burning. You can use 1 tablespoon oil and 1 tablespoon butter as a substitute. It will reach a good sautéing temperature without burning.

Condensed Milk Sweetened condensed milk plays an important part in Keys cooking. It is not the same as evaporated milk and the two are not interchangeable in recipes.

In an era when refrigeration was scarce and many cows were unhealthy and infected with disease, sweetened condensed milk was a major source of wholesome milk. In 1853, Gail Borden, considered the father of the modern dairy industry, perfected the method of extracting water from milk and adding sugar as a preservative. Sweetened condensed milk is a blend of whole milk and pure cane sugar with sixty percent of the water removed under vacuum. It has a thick, creamy consistency. Used to feed the Union Army during the Civil War, it was also popular for infant feeding until 1938, when doctors started prescribing baby formulas. During World War II, sweetened condensed milk was used in dessert recipes because sugar was scarce.

Sweetened condensed milk naturally thickens with the addition of an acid such as Key limes. Unopened, it keeps indefinitely.

Cuban Bananas Short fat bananas can be found in Latin markets or growing in South Dade and the Keys. They're called Cuban bananas, apple bananas, or sometimes finger bananas. They're juicier and sweeter than regular or Cavendish bananas. They taste a little bit like an apple and are very delicious. Regular bananas can be used as a substitute.

Evaporated Milk Evaporated milk is whole milk from which the water has been removed, but to which no sugar has been added. It is not interchangeable in recipes with sweetened condensed

milk. When an acid such as lemon or lime juice is mixed with evaporated milk, the milk curdles, making it unfit for use in such recipes as Key lime pie.

Guava and Guava Paste Guava is native to tropical America and was used as a fruit when the Europeans arrived in the late fifteenth and early sixteenth centuries. It has since spread throughout the tropical world. The fruit is a rich source of vitamin C and can be round or oblong in shape. The flesh has an intense flavor and a meaty texture. Because of its large pectin content it can be easily made into a paste which many cooks prefer because of its concentrated flavor and ease of use. The paste can be found in cans or long, narrow boxes in most supermarkets. Substitute guava jelly or, if this is unavailable, try a quince or red currant jelly. Guava can be eaten fresh, served with cream and sugar, used in shortcakes or fruit salads, or made into juice.

Hearts of Palm See Swamp Cabbage.

Key Limes The shrubby Key lime tree, *Citrus aurantifolio,* with its thorny branches grows to about fifteen feet. It is believed to have come from the sour orange tree and to have been brought to this hemisphere from the East Indies.

Some say that Dr. Henry Perrine, Governor-General of Indian Key in the 1830's, brought the tree to the Keys from Mexico; others believe it was transported by the Spanish and planted in the eighteenth century. Whichever way it came, it flourished in the Keys climate. It grows true from seeds and does not need grafting.

Key limes are yellow and look like small lemons. A Key lime pie should be a very pale yellow, not green. When making a pie with true Key limes, it will set immediately without any gelatin because of the high acid content of the lime. Most native Key limes sold in the markets now come from private homes or orchards. Citrus canker greatly curtailed the South Florida crop, although the disease is now under control. Commercial Key limes from Haiti are now being distributed year-round throughout the United States. Persian limes or green limes can be substituted in the Key lime recipes.

Malanga Malanga is a tropical root vegetable and an important source of carbohydrates and protein for many tropical cultures. It can be peeled and cooked like a potato. Since its cooked white flesh is slightly sweeter and nuttier in flavor than potatoes, it is often seasoned with just salt and pepper. It is available year-round.

Mamey Native to South America, this unusual fruit has a soft, salmon-pink flesh and a rough, russet-brown skin. Some say it tastes like sweet pumpkin, while true devotees say no other fruit can compare with it. Mamey has a texture similar to that of an avocado. It makes a delicious guacamole and will not turn dark. It is most often used in milk shakes but can also be peeled and eaten with a spoon or with a little cream and sugar.

Mango A native of southern Asia for at least 4,000 years, the mango has been cultivated in South Florida since the early 1800's. Florida mangoes may range from one-half pound to several pounds. There are now many varieties, all coming into season between May and September. Its flavor has been described as a blend of peach, apricot, and pineapple, but in reality, its rich flavor is all its own. Mangoes are wonderful just eaten plain. The cubed flesh is a great addition to chicken salads or as a complement to meat and vegetables dishes. Peaches may be used as a substitute in most recipes. Unripe mangoes make excellent chutneys.

To make mango cubes, hold the mango upright with the narrow side facing you. With a sharp knife slice off each side of the mango as close to the seed as possible. Peel the section containing the seed and cut off as much fruit as is possible. Hold the other two portions peel side down and score the fruit down to the peel in a tic-tac-toe fashion. Hold each scored portion with both hands and bend the peel backward. The cubes will stick up like porcupine needles. Draw your knife across the peel to remove the cubes. Repeat for the other portion. Serve the cubes or puree them for such desserts as puddings and sorbets.

Mile Marker The Keys stretch for about 165 miles from the mainland to the tip of Key West. There is a road running from Key Largo to Key West that is about 106 miles long. The railroad first placed mile markers, little white signs with green numbers, along the road with mile marker 1 in Key West and mile marker 105 in Key Largo. Today, most directions are given by mile marker number.

Old Bay This seasoning is used for steaming or poaching shellfish. It is a blend of spices including celery salt, mustard, pepper, bay leaf, cloves, allspice, ginger, mace, cardamom, cassia, and paprika.

Old Sour This sauce seems to be a native of Key West, where it is used sparingly as a condiment, on fish or chicken. In Cuba it is used as a marinade or in cooking. It was probably first made to use up Key limes and to have a supply of the juice when the limes were out of season. To

make it, add 1 tablespoon of salt to 2 cups of lime juice. Let sit at least two weeks in the refrigerator. It will keep for several weeks. Some people like to make their Old Sour hot by adding 2 bird peppers to the sauce. These tiny red or green peppers are about 1 inch long and are very hot. Use any type of chili pepper or hot sauce for your Old Sour.

Papaya Papaya, also known as pawpaw, has been part of the tropical diet for centuries. Christopher Columbus wrote in his journal that when he landed he noticed the natives of the West Indies eating a "tree melon" called "the fruit of the angels." It is a native of the Caribbean area and is grown in Florida. Papayas come in a variety of shapes and colors, the flesh ranging from pale yellow to golden orange. The new Caribbean Sunrise strain has been developed so that they can be picked when nearly ripe and are a rich red-orange color. These have a flowery fragrance that makes the papaya a special treat. They are available year-round. When green, the papaya is boiled or cut in half and baked like squash. Ripe papayas can be pureed for dressings, cooked with meat and poultry, served in fruit salads, or poached for desserts. The papaya remains firm when cooked.

Passion Fruit Passion fruit is one of the most fragrant of all edible fruits. The scent and sharp-sweet taste survive picking, packing, and transport. This fruit is a native of Brazil, but is now grown in many other hot climates, including Florida. Spanish Jesuit missionaries in South America saw the Signs of the Passion in each of the complex passion flowers. They believed the Creator had thoughtfully placed the flower in the New World to help with the conversion of the Indians. Hence the name passion fruit.

The small, round passion fruit can be pink, purple, or yellow-green. Wrinkling is a natural ripening characteristic. You can cut off the top of a ripe fruit and eat the pulp and seeds with a spoon; add some fresh cream, if you like. The seeds are pleasantly crunchy. Usually, however, the pulp is strained and used to flavor punches, hot tea, or sorbets and ice creams. The juice is used in tropical drinks and has been blended into a liqueur.

Pigeon Peas Pigeon peas are small round seeds about the size of regular peas. They can be bought either frozen or canned.

Pink Shrimp Sometimes called Pink Gold, these pink-shelled, juicy, large shrimp are part of the important Keys shrimping industry. They remain pink when cooked. They're delicious, and cooking with them produces wonderful recipes. Any good quality large shrimp can be substituted in the recipes.

Plantain The plantain is a member of the banana family and looks like an oversize banana. When they are green, they are hard and starchy and are used very much like a potato or sliced and fried for plantain chips. As they ripen, they turn yellow and then black, and develop more of a sweet banana flavor, but they hold their shape better than bananas when cooked. Peeling a plantain is a little tricky, as the peel wants to stick to the flesh. Take a knife and slice the skin along the natural ridges of the plantain. Then peel the strips away. If you have a yellow plantain that is not quite ripe yet, place it in a 300-degree oven until it turns black and the skin begins to split. This only works with plantains that have already started to turn yellow. Bananas can be substituted for plantains in recipes, but they are softer and should be handled carefully during cooking.

Saffron These delicate yellow strands are the dried stigmas of a saffron crocus, *Crocus sativus*. They must be picked out of each flower by hand. It takes three to four hundred thousand flowers to make one pound of dried saffron. Used in sauces and soups, saffron imparts a delicate perfumed flavor and yellow color. Bijol or tumeric can be used as a substitute.

Sofrito Sofrito is a basic Spanish sauce that is used to give added depth of flavor in many Cuban recipes. It usually has onions, garlic, green pepper, tomatoes, spices, and sometimes ham. All of the ingredients are cooked in oil.

Sour Oranges Bitter or sour orange, *Citrus aurantium,* is in all probability the ancestor of all oranges. It is the hardiest type of orange and is better for cooking than the sweet orange. It grows true from seed, where the sweeter varieties do not. Sweet oranges are probably mutants of bitter oranges. China is considered to be the home of origin of the orange. According to Waverly Root, in 1500 B.C., I Yin, Minister of the Emperor Ch'eng T'ang, recommended "the bitter orange of Chiang-pu." It is thought that the orange was brought to Rome by Arabs and then to North Africa and Spain. Christopher Columbus brought oranges to the New World, and the climate of the West Indies helped orange groves flourish. The first oranges brought to the Caribbean were probably sour oranges, and it is these that figure so importantly in Latin cooking. If you do not have sour oranges, then use half sweet orange juice and half lime juice as a substitute.

Swamp Cabbage (Hearts of Palm) This interesting vegetable has two names. Call it swamp cabbage and it connotes down-home cooking. Use its other name, hearts of palm, and it could be served at the Ritz. The swamp cabbage by any name is the inner core of the palm tree that also contains the heart. The center of the palm tree grows in concentric rings, looking something like an onion cut in half. The palm is trimmed until the tender center is reached. This is the area that can be broken off with your fingers. Beyond this part is the dense, tightly knit section, or the heart. If the tree is more than eight to ten feet tall or too near the water, the core will be bitter. Fresh hearts of palm are difficult to find. They should be very sweet and crunchy. Canned hearts of palm are now sold in supermarkets. They can be served in a salad or cooked as a vegetable.

Acknowledgments and List of Restaurants

This book is based on ideas and recipes from every corner of the Florida Keys. Meeting and talking with people who shared their knowledge made this a very special project for me. What would I have done without the extraordinary efforts of this exceptional team?

A very special thanks to my husband, Harold, who not only encouraged me and gave advice, but who assisted in devising these recipes and spent endless hours helping me edit my book.

Additional thanks to:

Carl Navarre, who conceived the idea for *Keys Cuisine* and encouraged me to research this area of the United States that he loves so much.

Kitty Clements, who introduced me to everyone she knew, helped organize my visits to Key West, and has more energy than even I do; and to her husband, Tom, who waited patiently for his dinners while I questioned everyone in sight.

Joy and Stanley Jaffee, who rushed to my aid when my computer chips were down.

Jim Boilini and his Key Largo Island Jubilee Cook-Off, where I met and interviewed so many of the Upper Keys cooks.

And to the following restaurants and people in the Keys who opened their doors for me:

In **Key Largo**: Debbie and Rick Alvarez at *Tugboat Annie's,* Mary Ballard from *Ganim's* restaurant, Craig Belcher from *Craig's Restaurant,* Don Chrzan of *Mary and Stan's* restaurant, Dottie Hill of *Key Largo Fisheries,* Pam Manresa of *Gardener's Market,* Gerri and Barry Richman at the *Hideout,* and Pat Mathias and Karen Punturo at *Snook's Bayside Club.*

In **Windley Key**: Marc Green at the *Holiday Isle Restaurant.*

In **Plantation Key**: André Mueller of *Marker 88.*

In **Islamorada**: Dorothy Hertel and Claudette Becker of the *Islamorada Fish Company,* John Maloughney at the *Lorelei Restaurant,* Manny and Isa Ortiz at *Manny and Isa's Restaurant,* Henry Rosenthal at the *Green Turtle Inn,* Dawn Sieber and Susan Waterman of *Cheeca Lodge,* Margaret Stevens of *Lovin' Dough, Inc.,* Virginia and Alan Stocki and Henri Champagne at *Ziggie's The Conch.*

In **Duck Key**: George Boyer of *Hawk's Cay Resort and Marina.*

In **Little Torch Key**: Michel Reymond at *Little Palm Island.*

In **Summerland**: Mike Montalto at *Monte's Seafood.*

In **Key West**: Charlene Borck and Kathy Lewis at the *Waterfront Fish Market,* Bruce Cernicky of *Nick's Upstairs Bar and Restaurant* at the Hyatt, Tim Duffy of *Sloppy Joe's Bar,* Bill Gaiser at the *Carriage Trade Garden,* Edna Howard and the *Cornish Memorial AME Church,* Michael Kulow of *The Pier House,* Claude Lucas of *Croissants de France,* Tom McCutchen at *Garrison Bite,* Bertha Mira at *B's Restaurant,* Herderito Paez at *5 Brothers Grocery,* Diane Pansire of *Rich's Cafe* in the *Eden House,* Karole Rispoli and the bartender Glen at *Ocean Key House,* Ellen Rochford at *The Top at La Concha,* Doug Shook and Justin at *Louie's Backyard,* Paige at the *Hog's Breath Saloon,* Michael and Steve from the *Roof Top Café,* the ladies of the *St. James Missionary Baptist Church,* and the folks at *La Te Da, La Terraza de Marti, Kyushu, La Lechonera, Full Moon Saloon, Ocean Reef Club,* and the *Casa Marina.*

And to the following people throughout the Keys who generously shared their recipes with me: Susan Craig and Laurie Richards, Margaret Dicker, Lois and John Ebert (Tiki John), Gary Ellis, founder of the Redbone Celebrity Tournament, Bob and Clara Hardin, Linda Haywood, Kathy Hughson, Sis Kelm and Bec Washington, George Hommel, Billy Knowles, Tom McGuane, Bobbie Sawyer, Reta Sawyer, Mary Spottswood, Sally Thomas, Norman Van Aken, Eddie Wightman, Helen Willensky, and Mitchell Wolfson, Jr.

Index

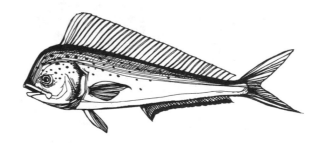